D0446636

Steps to Christ
for
A Sanctified Life

E. G. White

Printed by
Remnant Publications, Inc.

Cover art by Harry Anderson
© Review and Herald Publishing Association

Steps to Christ for a Sanctified Life

This edition published 2005

© Copyright by
The Ellen G. White Publications

Printed in the United States of America
All Rights Reserved

ISBN 1-883012-59-7

A Note From the Publisher

Steps to Christ for a Sanctified Life brings together in one volume, two classic Christian books previously published as *Steps to Christ* and *The Sanctified Life.*

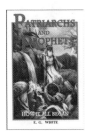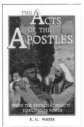

What makes this set so popular?
The Results!
Lifechanging Results
The Bible Study Companion Set *$59.95

All five books together covering Genesis to Revelation—from the beginning of the universe through human history and on into our future. This set truly enriches your life with a better understanding of the Bible.

Patriarchs and Prophets
Where did the human race come from? Why do bad things happen to good people? Why are babies born sick, and why do so many hard-working people never seem to get ahead? If God is good, why doesn't He prevent sadness and heartbreak? And if He is allpowerful, why doesn't He do something about evil and sickness? These questions and many more are answered in this remarkable book. *Patriarchs and Prophets* has brought peace and hope to millions throughout the world.   US$11.99

Prophets and Kings
Beginning with King Solomon, this book recounts the stories of great men and women of the Bible who lived from his reign to the first advent of Jesus Christ. Here you will read of Elijah, Daniel, Isaiah, and Jeremiah, among others—and you will find the lessons God would have us all learn from their lives. US$11.99

The Desire of Ages
This book is about the Man who stands at the center of all human history. No one else has had such a profound influence on the people of this planet as Jesus Christ. US$11.99

The Acts of the Apostles
This book is about power—ultimate power. The awesome power of the Holy Spirit, and what He can do in human lives when we surrender to be used by Him. When Pentecost came upon the early church, what God's people accomplished was miraculous. And all that the apostles did, God wants to do again through us today. US$11.99

The Great Controversy
The world is on the verge of a stupendous crises. Here is the authoritative answer to the confusion and despair of this tense age. Revealing God's ultimate plan for mankind. *The Great Controversy* may be the most important book you'll ever read. US$11.99

These three books
will change your life...
...Forever
The Life-Giving Secrets Set $29.95

This three volume set will help you in your understanding the whole being—Physical, mental, and spiritual. With over 2,200 spiritual references, this set will make it simple to understand these Life—giving secrets.

Living the Life of the Lifegiver
Here is the most compelling book ever written on the parables of Jesus. Through familiar objects and incidents—the harvest, the shepherd, the builder, the traveler, the homemaker—Jesus linked divine truth with the common and ordinary. As you read this book, you will experience the sensation of walking through a door into a previously unseen but very real world. US$9.95

Education
This book clearly reveals that love, the basis of creation and redemption, is the basis of true education. Simply put, changes that last are those that are motivated by unselfish love. US$9.95

The Ministry of Healing
Using Jesus Christ as the example of the true Medical Missionary, this book, first written over 80 years ago, is an extraordinary example of medical-science prophecy. Many topics, such as mind cures, natural remedies, vegetarian diet, exercise, prenatal influences, and health education, are covered. The author speaks of true health and healing in conjunction with the powers of the Great Physician, Jesus Christ. US$9.95

Credit card orders, call: 800-423-1319

Send check or money order to:
Remnant Publications
P.O. Box 426, Coldwater, MI 49036

CONCORDIA UNIVERSITY LIBRARY
PORTLAND, OR 97211

ARE YOU SEARCHING FOR TRUTH?

Do you need reliable answers to urgent questions?

- *Can we know and understand the future?*
- *What are the tests of a true prophet?*
- *Is the development of character important?*
- *Are there physical and spiritual laws for health and happiness?*
- *What really happens to us after death?*
- *Is it possible to live forever?*
- *How can you find inner peace in a world of chaos?*

Discover the answers to these and other vital questions by enrolling in our Bible Correspondence Course. We care about you and your welfare. Thats why we prepared this series of thought-provoking Bible study lessons to help people just like you. These lessons will stimulate you to think independently, and help you conscientiously make the choices which will make you happy.

The first two lessons in the series are free of charge. If you like the lessons, we ask you to include a nominal freewill offering, beginning with lesson three, to help cover postage and handling.

Do You Want To Know More?

Yes, Please send me, at no charge, the first two lessons.

Name _____

Address _____

City State _____ Zip _____

Send to:

**Bible Correspondence Course
P.O. Box 426
Coldwater, MI 49036**   SC 05

Contents

1

God's Love for Man

Nature and revelation alike testify of God's love. Our Father in heaven is the source of life, of wisdom, and of joy. Look at the wonderful and beautiful things of nature. Think of their marvelous adaptation to the needs and happiness, not only of man, but of all living creatures. The sunshine and the rain, that gladden and refresh the earth, the hills and seas and plains, all speak to us of the Creator's love. It is God who supplies the daily needs of all His creatures. In the beautiful words of the psalmist—

"The eyes of all wait upon Thee;
And Thou givest them their meat in due season.
Thou openest Thine hand,
And satisfiest the desire of every living thing."
Psalm 145:15, 16.

God made man perfectly holy and happy; and the fair earth, as it came from the Creator's hand, bore no blight of decay or shadow of the curse. It is transgression of God's law—the law of love—that has brought woe and death. Yet even amid the suffering that results from sin, God's love is revealed. It is written that God cursed the ground for man's sake. Genesis 3:17. The thorn and the thistle—the difficulties and trials that make his life one of toil and care—were appointed for his good as a part of the training needful in God's plan for his uplifting from the ruin and degradation that sin has wrought. The world, though fallen, is not all sorrow and misery. In nature itself are messages of hope and comfort. There are flowers upon the thistles, and the thorns are covered with roses.

"God is love" is written upon every opening bud, upon every spire of springing grass. The lovely birds making the air vocal with their happy songs, the delicately tinted flowers in their perfection perfuming the air, the lofty trees of the forest with their rich foliage of living green—all testify to the tender, fatherly care of our God and to His desire to make His children happy.

The word of God reveals His character. He Himself has declared His infinite love and pity. When Moses prayed, "Show me Thy glory," the Lord answered, "I will make all My goodness pass before thee." Exodus 33:18, 19. This is His glory. The Lord passed before Moses, and proclaimed, "The Lord, The Lord God, merciful and gracious, long-suffering, and abundant in goodness and truth, keeping mercy for thousands, forgiving iniquity and transgression and sin." Exodus 34:6, 7. He is "slow to anger, and of great kindness," "because He delighteth in mercy." Jonah 4:2; Micah 7:18.

God has bound our hearts to Him by unnumbered tokens in heaven and in earth. Through the things of nature, and the deepest and tenderest earthly ties that human hearts can know, He has sought to reveal Himself to us. Yet these but imperfectly represent His love. Though all these evidences have been given, the enemy of good blinded the minds of men, so that they looked upon God with fear; they thought of Him as severe and unforgiving. Satan led men to conceive of God as a being whose chief attribute is stern justice,—one who is a severe judge, a harsh, exacting creditor. He pictured the Creator as a being who is watching with jealous eye to discern the errors and mistakes of men, that He may visit judgments upon them. It was to remove this dark shadow, by revealing to the world the infinite love of God, that Jesus came to live among men.

The Son of God came from heaven to make manifest the Father. "No man hath seen God at any time; the only begotten Son, which is in the bosom of the Father, He hath declared Him." John 1:18. "Neither knoweth any man the Father, save the Son, and he to whomsoever the Son will reveal Him." Matthew 11:27. When one of the disciples made the request, "Show us the Father," Jesus answered, "Have I been so long time with you, and yet hast thou not known Me, Philip? He that hath seen Me hath seen the Father; and how sayest thou then, Show us the Father?" John 14:8, 9.

In describing His earthly mission, Jesus said, The Lord "hath anointed Me to preach the gospel to the poor; He hath sent Me to heal the brokenhearted, to preach deliverance to the captives, and recovering of sight to the blind, to set at liberty them that are bruised." Luke 4:18. This was His work. He went about doing good and healing all that were oppressed by Satan. There were whole villages where there was not a moan of sickness in any house, for He had passed through them and healed all their sick. His work gave evidence of His divine anointing. Love, mercy, and compassion were revealed in every act of His life; His heart went out in tender sympathy to the children of men. He took man's nature, that He might reach man's wants. The poorest and humblest were not afraid to approach Him. Even little children were attracted to Him. They loved to climb upon His knees and gaze into the pensive face, benignant with love.

Jesus did not suppress one word of truth, but He uttered it always in love. He exercised the greatest tact and thoughtful, kind attention in His intercourse with the people. He was never rude, never needlessly spoke a severe word, never gave needless pain to a sensitive soul. He did not censure human weakness. He spoke the truth, but always in love. He denounced hypocrisy, unbelief, and iniquity; but tears were in His voice as He uttered His scathing rebukes. He wept over Jerusalem, the city He loved, which refused to receive Him, the way, the truth, and the life. They had rejected Him, the Saviour, but He regarded them with pitying tenderness. His life was one of self-denial and thoughtful care for others. Every soul was precious in His eyes. While He ever bore Himself with divine dignity, He bowed with the tenderest regard to every member of the family of God. In all men He saw fallen souls whom it was His mission to save.

Such is the character of Christ as revealed in His life. This is the character of God. It is from the Father's heart that the streams of divine compassion, manifest in Christ, flow out to the children of men. Jesus, the tender, pitying Saviour, was God "manifest in the flesh." 1 Timothy 3:16.

It was to redeem us that Jesus lived and suffered and died. He became "a Man of Sorrows," that we might be made partakers of everlasting joy. God permitted His beloved Son, full of grace and truth, to come from a world of indescribable glory, to a world marred and blighted with sin, darkened with the shadow of death and the curse. He permitted Him to leave the bosom of His love, the adoration of the angels, to suffer shame, insult, humiliation, hatred, and death. "The chastisement of our peace was upon Him; and with His stripes we are healed." Isaiah 53:5. Behold Him in the wilderness, in Gethsemane, upon the cross! The spotless Son of God took upon Himself the burden of sin. He who had been one with God, felt in His soul the awful separation that sin makes between God and man. This wrung from His lips the anguished cry, "My God, My God, why hast Thou forsaken Me?" Matthew 27:46. It was the burden of sin, the sense of its terrible enormity, of its separation of the soul from God—it was this that broke the heart of the Son of God.

But this great sacrifice was not made in order to create in the Father's heart a love for man, not to make Him willing to save. No, no! "God so loved the world, that He gave His only-begotten Son." John 3:16. The Father loves us, not because of the great propitiation, but He provided the propitiation because He loves us. Christ was the medium through which He could pour out His infinite love upon a fallen world. "God was in Christ, reconciling the world unto Himself." 2 Corinthians 5:19. God suffered with His Son. In the agony of Gethsemane, the death of Calvary, the heart of Infinite Love paid the price of our redemption.

Jesus said, "Therefore doth My Father love Me, because I lay down My life, that I might take it again." John 10:17. That is, "My Father has so loved you that He even loves Me more for giving My life to redeem you. In becoming your Substitute and Surety, by surrendering My life, by taking your liabilities, your transgressions, I am endeared to My Father; for by My sacrifice, God can be just, and yet the Justifier of him who believeth in Jesus."

None but the Son of God could accomplish our redemption; for only He who was in the bosom of the Father could declare Him. Only He who knew the height and depth of the love of God could make it manifest. Nothing less than the infinite sacrifice made by Christ in behalf of fallen man could express the Father's love to lost humanity.

"God so loved the world, that He gave His only-begotten Son." He gave Him not only to live among men, to bear their sins, and die their sacrifice. He gave Him to the fallen race. Christ was to identify Himself with the interests and needs of humanity. He who was one with God has linked Himself with the children of men by ties that are never to be broken. Jesus is "not ashamed to call them brethren" (Hebrews 2:11); He is our Sacrifice, our Advocate, our

Brother, bearing our human form before the Father's throne, and through eternal ages one with the race He has redeemed—the Son of man. And all this that man might be uplifted from the ruin and degradation of sin that he might reflect the love of God and share the joy of holiness.

The price paid for our redemption, the infinite sacrifice of our heavenly Father in giving His Son to die for us, should give us exalted conceptions of what we may become through Christ. As the inspired apostle John beheld the height, the depth, the breadth of the Father's love toward the perishing race, he was filled with adoration and reverence; and, failing to find suitable language in which to express the greatness and tenderness of this love, he called upon the world to behold it. "Behold, what manner of love the Father hath bestowed upon us, that we should be called the sons of God." 1 John 3:1. What a value this places upon man! Through transgression the sons of man become subjects of Satan. Through faith in the atoning sacrifice of Christ the sons of Adam may become the sons of God. By assuming human nature, Christ elevates humanity. Fallen men are placed where, through connection with Christ, they may indeed become worthy of the name "sons of God."

Such love is without a parallel. Children of the heavenly King! Precious promise! Theme for the most profound meditation! The matchless love of God for a world that did not love Him! The thought has a subduing power upon the soul and brings the mind into captivity to the will of God. The more we study the divine character in the light of the cross, the more we see mercy, tenderness, and forgiveness blended with equity and justice, and the more clearly we discern innumerable evidences of a love that is infinite and a tender pity surpassing a mother's yearning sympathy for her wayward child.

2
The Sinner's Need of Christ

Man was originally endowed with noble powers and a well-balanced mind. He was perfect in his being, and in harmony with God. His thoughts were pure, his aims holy. But through disobedience, his powers were perverted, and selfishness took the place of love. His nature became so weakened through transgression that it was impossible for him, in his own strength, to resist the power of evil. He was made captive by Satan, and would have remained so forever had not God specially interposed. It was the tempter's purpose to thwart the divine plan in man's creation, and fill the earth with woe and desolation. And he would point to all this evil as the result of God's work in creating man.

In his sinless state, man held joyful communion with Him "in whom are hid all the treasures of wisdom and knowledge." Colossians 2:3. But after his sin, he could no longer find joy in holiness, and he sought to hide from the presence of God. Such is still the condition of the unrenewed heart. It is not in harmony with God, and finds no joy in communion with Him. The sinner could not be happy in God's presence; he would shrink from the companionship of holy beings. Could he be permitted to enter heaven, it would have no joy for him. The spirit of unselfish love that reigns there—every heart responding to the heart of Infinite Love—would touch no answering chord in his soul. His thoughts, his interests, his motives, would be alien to those that actuate the sinless dwellers there. He would be a discordant note in the melody of heaven. Heaven would be to him a place of torture; he would long to be hidden from Him who is its light, and the center of its joy. It is no arbitrary decree on the part of God that excludes the wicked from heaven; they are shut out by their own unfitness for its companionship. The glory of God would be to them a consuming fire. They would welcome destruction, that they might be hidden from the face of Him who died to redeem them.

It is impossible for us, of ourselves, to escape from the pit of sin in which we are sunken. Our hearts are evil, and we cannot change them. "Who can bring a clean thing out of an unclean? not one." "The carnal mind is enmity against God: for it is not subject to the law of God, neither indeed can be." Job 14:4; Romans 8:7. Education, culture, the exercise of the will, human effort, all have their proper sphere, but here they are powerless. They may produce an outward correctness of behavior, but they cannot change the heart; they cannot purify the springs of life. There must be a power working from within, a new life from above, before men can be changed from sin to holiness. That power is Christ. His grace alone can quicken the lifeless faculties of the soul, and attract it to God, to holiness.

The Saviour said, "Except a man be born from above," unless he shall receive a new heart, new desires, purposes, and motives, leading to a new life, "he cannot see the kingdom of God." John 3:3, margin. The idea that it is necessary only to develop the good that exists in man by nature, is a fatal deception. "The natural man receiveth not the things of the Spirit of God: for they are foolishness unto him: neither can he know them, because they are spiritually discerned." "Marvel not that I said unto thee, Ye must be born again." 1 Corinthians 2:14; John 3:7. Of Christ it is written, "In Him was life; and the life was the light of men"—the only "name under heaven given among men, whereby we must be saved." John 1:4; Acts 4:12.

It is not enough to perceive the loving-kindness of God, to see the benevolence, the fatherly tenderness, of His character. It is not enough to discern the wisdom and justice of His law, to see that it is founded upon the eternal principle of love. Paul the apostle saw all this when he exclaimed, "I consent unto the law that it is good." "The law is holy, and the commandment holy, and just, and good." But he added, in the bitterness of his soul-anguish and despair, "I am carnal, sold under sin." Romans 7:16, 12, 14. He longed for the purity, the righteousness, to which in himself he was powerless to attain, and cried out, "O wretched man that I am! who shall deliver me from this body of death?" Romans 7:24, margin. Such is the cry that has gone up from burdened hearts in all lands and in all ages. To all, there is but one answer, "Behold the Lamb of God, which taketh away the sin of the world." John 1:29.

Many are the figures by which the Spirit of God has sought to illustrate this truth, and make it plain to souls that long to be freed from the burden of guilt. When, after his sin in deceiving Esau, Jacob fled from his father's home, he was weighed down with a sense of guilt. Lonely and outcast as he was, separated from all that had made life dear, the one thought that above all others pressed upon his soul, was the fear that his sin had cut him off from God, that he was forsaken of Heaven. In sadness he lay down to rest on the bare earth, around him only the lonely hills, and above, the heavens bright with stars. As he slept, a strange light broke upon his vision; and lo, from the plain on which he lay, vast shadowy stairs seemed to lead upward to the very gates of heaven, and upon them angels of God were passing up and down; while from the glory above, the divine voice was heard in a message of comfort and hope. Thus was made known to Jacob that which met the need and longing of his soul—a Saviour. With joy and gratitude he saw revealed a way by which he, a sinner, could be restored to communion with God. The mystic ladder of his dream represented Jesus, the only medium of communication between God and man.

This is the same figure to which Christ referred in His conversation with Nathanael, when He said, "Ye shall see heaven open, and the angels of God ascending and descending upon the Son of man." John 1:51. In the apostasy, man alienated himself from God; earth was cut off from heaven. Across the gulf that lay between, there could be no communion. But through Christ, earth is again linked with heaven. With His own merits, Christ has bridged the gulf which sin had made, so that the ministering angels can hold communion with man. Christ connects fallen man in his weakness and helplessness with the Source of infinite power.

But in vain are men's dreams of progress, in vain all efforts for the uplifting of humanity, if they neglect the one Source of hope and help for the fallen race. "Every good gift and every perfect gift" (James 1:17) is from God. There is no true excellence of character apart from Him. And the only way to God is Christ. He says, "I am the way, the truth, and the life: no man cometh unto the Father, but by Me." John 14:6.

The heart of God yearns over His earthly children with a love stronger than death. In giving up His Son, He has poured out to us all heaven in one gift. The Saviour's life and death and intercession, the ministry of angels, the pleading of the Spirit, the Father working above and through all, the unceasing interest of heavenly beings,—all are enlisted in behalf of man's redemption.

Oh, let us contemplate the amazing sacrifice that has been made for us! Let us try to appreciate the labor and energy that Heaven is expending to reclaim the lost, and bring them back to the Father's house. Motives stronger, and agencies more powerful, could never be brought into operation; the exceeding rewards for right-doing, the enjoyment of heaven, the society of the angels, the communion and love of God and His Son, the elevation and extension of all our powers throughout eternal ages—are these not mighty incentives and encouragements to urge us to give the heart's loving service to our Creator and Redeemer?

And, on the other hand, the judgments of God pronounced against sin, the inevitable retribution, the degradation of our character, and the final destruction, are presented in God's word to warn us against the service of Satan.

Shall we not regard the mercy of God? What more could He do? Let us place ourselves in right relation to Him who has loved us with amazing love. Let us avail ourselves of the means provided for us that we may be transformed into His likeness, and be restored to fellowship with the ministering angels, to harmony and communion with the Father and the Son.

3
Repentance

How shall a man be just with God? How shall the sinner be made righteous? It is only through Christ that we can be brought into harmony with God, with holiness; but how are we to come to Christ? Many are asking the same question as did the multitude on the Day of Pentecost, when, convicted of sin, they cried out, "What shall we do?" The first word of Peter's answer was, "Repent." Acts 2:37, 38. At another time, shortly after, he said, "Repent, . . . and be converted, that your sins may be blotted out." Acts 3:19.

Repentance includes sorrow for sin and a turning away from it. We shall not renounce sin unless we see its sinfulness; until we turn away from it in heart, there will be no real change in the life.

There are many who fail to understand the true nature of repentance. Multitudes sorrow that they have sinned and even make an outward reformation because they fear that their wrongdoing will bring suffering upon themselves. But this is not repentance in the Bible sense. They lament the suffering rather than the sin. Such was the grief of Esau when he saw that the birthright was lost to him forever. Balaam, terrified by the angel standing in his pathway with drawn sword, acknowledged his guilt lest he should lose his life; but there was no genuine repentance for sin, no conversion of purpose, no abhorrence of evil. Judas Iscariot, after betraying his Lord, exclaimed, "I have sinned in that I have betrayed the innocent blood." Matthew 27:4.

The confession was forced from his guilty soul by an awful sense of condemnation and a fearful looking for of judgment. The consequences that were to result to him filled him with terror, but there was no deep, heartbreaking grief in his soul, that he had betrayed the spotless Son of God and denied the Holy One of Israel. Pharaoh, when suffering under the judgments of God, acknowledged his sin in order to escape further punishment, but returned to his defiance of Heaven as soon as the plagues were stayed. These all lamented the results of sin, but did not sorrow for the sin itself.

But when the heart yields to the influence of the Spirit of God, the conscience will be quickened, and the sinner will discern something of the depth and sacredness of God's holy law, the foundation of His government in heaven and on earth. The "Light, which lighteth every man that cometh into the world," illumines the secret chambers of the soul, and the hidden things of darkness are made manifest. John 1:9. Conviction takes hold upon the mind and heart. The sinner has a sense of the righteousness of Jehovah and feels the terror of appearing, in his own guilt and uncleanness, before the Searcher of hearts. He sees the love of God, the beauty of holiness, the joy of purity; he longs to be cleansed and to be restored to communion with Heaven.

The prayer of David after his fall, illustrates the nature of true sorrow for sin. His repentance was sincere and deep. There was no effort to palliate his guilt; no desire to escape the judgment threatened, inspired his prayer. David saw the enormity of his transgression; he saw the defilement of his soul; he loathed his sin. It was not for pardon only that he prayed, but for purity of heart. He longed for the joy of holiness—to be restored to harmony and communion with God. This was the language of his soul:

> "Blessed is he whose transgression is forgiven,
> whose sin is covered.
> Blessed is the man unto whom the Lord
> imputeth not iniquity,
> And in whose spirit there is no guile."
>   Psalm 32:1, 2.
> "Have mercy upon me, O God, according to
> Thy loving-kindness:
> According unto the multitude of Thy tender
> mercies blot out my transgressions. . . .
> For I acknowledge my transgressions: and my
> sin is ever before me. . . .
> Purge me with hyssop, and I shall be clean:
> wash me, and I shall be whiter than snow. . . .
> Create in me a clean heart, O God;
> And renew a right spirit within me.
> Cast me not away from Thy presence;
> And take not Thy Holy Spirit from me.
> Restore unto me the joy of Thy salvation;
> And uphold me with Thy free spirit. . . .
> Deliver me from bloodguiltiness, O God, Thou
> God of my salvation:
> And my tongue shall sing aloud of Thy
> righteousness."   Psalm 51:1-14.

A repentance such as this, is beyond the reach of our own power to accomplish; it is obtained only from Christ, who ascended up on high and has given gifts unto men.

Just here is a point on which many may err, and hence they fail of receiving the help that Christ desires to give them. They think that they cannot come to Christ unless they first repent, and that repentance prepares for the forgiveness of their sins. It is true that repentance does precede the forgiveness of sins; for it is only the broken and contrite heart that will feel the need of a Saviour. But must the sinner wait till he has repented before he can come to Jesus? Is repentance to be made an obstacle between the sinner and the Saviour?

The Bible does not teach that the sinner must repent before he can heed the invitation of Christ, "Come unto Me, all ye that labor and are heavy-laden, and I will give you rest." Matthew 11:28. It is the virtue that goes forth from Christ, that leads to genuine repentance. Peter made the matter clear in his statement to the Israelites when he said, "Him hath God exalted with His right hand to be a Prince and a Saviour, for to give repentance to Israel, and forgiveness of sins." Acts 5:31. We can no more repent without the Spirit of Christ to awaken the conscience than we can be pardoned without Christ.

Christ is the source of every right impulse. He is the only one that can implant in the heart enmity against sin. Every desire for truth and purity, every conviction of our own sinfulness, is an evidence that His Spirit is moving upon our hearts.

Jesus has said, "I, if I be lifted up from the earth, will draw all men unto Me." John 12:32. Christ must be revealed to the sinner as the Saviour dying for the sins of the world; and as we behold the Lamb of God upon the cross of Calvary, the mystery of redemption begins to unfold to our minds and the goodness of God leads us to repentance. In dying for sinners, Christ manifested a love that is incomprehensible; and as the sinner beholds this love, it softens the heart, impresses the mind, and inspires contrition in the soul.

It is true that men sometimes become ashamed of their sinful ways, and give up some of their evil habits, before they are conscious that they are being drawn to Christ. But whenever they make an effort to reform, from a sincere desire to do right, it is the power of Christ that is drawing them. An influence of which they are unconscious works upon the soul, and the conscience is quickened, and the outward life is amended. And as Christ draws them to look upon His cross, to behold Him whom their sins have pierced, the commandment comes home to the conscience. The wickedness of their life, the deepseated sin of the soul, is revealed to them. They begin to comprehend something of the righteousness of Christ, and exclaim, "What is sin, that it should require such a sacrifice for the redemption of its victim? Was all this love, all this suffering, all this humiliation, demanded, that we might not perish, but have everlasting life?"

The sinner may resist this love, may refuse to be drawn to Christ; but if he does not resist he will be drawn to Jesus; a knowledge of the plan of salvation will lead him to the foot of the cross in repentance for his sins, which have caused the sufferings of God's dear Son.

The same divine mind that is working upon the things of nature is speaking to the hearts of men and creating an inexpressible craving for something they have not. The things of the world cannot satisfy their longing. The Spirit of God is pleading with them to seek for those things that alone can give peace and rest—the grace of Christ, the joy of holiness. Through influences seen and unseen, our Saviour is constantly at work to attract the minds of men from the unsatisfying pleasures of sin to the infinite blessings that may be theirs in Him. To all these souls, who are vainly seeking to drink from the broken cisterns of this world, the divine message is addressed, "Let him that is athirst come. And whosoever will, let him take the water of life freely." Revelation 22:17.

You who in heart long for something better than this world can give, recognize this longing as the voice of God to your soul. Ask Him to give you repentance, to reveal Christ to you in His infinite love, in His perfect purity. In the Saviour's life the principles of God's law—love to God and man—were perfectly exemplified. Benevolence, unselfish love, was the life of His soul. It is as we behold Him, as the light from our Saviour falls upon us, that we see the sinfulness of our own hearts.

We may have flattered ourselves, as did Nicodemus, that our life has been upright, that our moral character is correct, and think that we need not humble the heart before God, like the common sinner: but when the light from Christ shines into our souls, we shall see how impure we are; we shall discern the selfishness of motive, the enmity against God, that has defiled every act of life. Then we shall know that our own righteousness is indeed as filthy rags, and that the blood of Christ alone can cleanse us from the defilement of sin, and renew our hearts in His own likeness.

One ray of the glory of God, one gleam of the purity of Christ, penetrating the soul, makes every spot of defilement painfully distinct, and lays bare the deformity and defects of the human character. It makes apparent the unhallowed desires, the infidelity of the heart, the impurity of the lips. The sinner's acts of disloyalty in making void the law of God, are exposed to his sight, and his spirit is stricken and afflicted under the searching influence of the Spirit of God. He loathes himself as he views the pure, spotless character of Christ.

When the prophet Daniel beheld the glory surrounding the heavenly messenger that was sent unto him, he was overwhelmed with a sense of his own weakness and imperfection. Describing the effect of the wonderful scene, he says, "There remained no strength in me: for my comeliness was turned in me into corruption, and I retained no strength." Daniel 10:8. The soul thus touched will hate its selfishness, abhor its self-love, and will seek, through Christ's righteousness, for the purity of heart that is in harmony with the law of God and the character of Christ.

Paul says that as "touching the righteousness which is in the law"—as far as outward acts were concerned—he was "blameless" (Philippians 3:6); but when the spiritual character of the law was discerned, he saw himself a sinner. Judged by the letter of the law as men apply it to the outward life, he had abstained from sin; but when he looked into the depths of its holy precepts, and saw himself as God saw him, he bowed in humiliation and confessed his guilt. He says, "I was alive without the law once: but when the commandment came, sin revived, and I died." Romans 7:9. When he saw the spiritual nature of the law, sin appeared in its true hideousness, and his self-esteem was gone.

God does not regard all sins as of equal magnitude; there are degrees of guilt in His estimation, as well as in that of man; but however trifling this or that wrong act may seem in the eyes of men, no sin is small in the sight of God. Man's judgment is partial, imperfect; but God estimates all things as they really are. The drunkard is despised and is told that his sin will exclude him from heaven; while pride, selfishness, and covetousness too often go unrebuked. But these are sins that are especially offensive to God; for they are contrary to the benevolence of His character, to that unselfish love which is the very atmosphere of the unfallen universe. He who falls into some of the grosser sins may feel a sense of his shame and poverty and his need of the grace of Christ; but pride feels no need, and so it closes the heart against Christ and the infinite blessings He came to give.

The poor publican who prayed, "God be merciful to me a sinner" (Luke 18:13), regarded himself as a very wicked man, and others looked upon him in the same light; but he felt his need, and with his burden of guilt and shame he came before God, asking for His mercy. His heart was open for the Spirit of God to do its gracious work and set him free from the power of sin. The Pharisee's boastful, self-righteous prayer showed that his heart was closed against the influence of the Holy Spirit. Because of his distance from God, he had no sense of his own defilement, in contrast with the perfection of the divine holiness. He felt no need, and he received nothing.

If you see your sinfulness, do not wait to make yourself better. How many there are who think they are not good enough to come to Christ. Do you expect to become better through your own efforts? "Can the Ethiopian change his skin, or the leopard his spots? then may ye also do good, that are accustomed to do evil." Jeremiah 13:23. There is help for us only in God. We must not wait for stronger persuasions, for better opportunities, or for holier tempers. We can do nothing of ourselves. We must come to Christ just as we are.

But let none deceive themselves with the thought that God, in His great love and mercy, will yet save even the rejecters of His grace. The exceeding sinfulness of sin can be estimated only in the light of the cross. When men urge that God is too good to cast off the sinner, let them look to Calvary. It was because there was no other way in which man could be saved, because without this sacrifice it was impossible for the human race to escape from the defiling power of sin, and be restored to communion with holy beings,—impossible for them again to become partakers of spiritual life,—it was because of this that Christ took upon Himself the guilt of the disobedient and suffered in the sinner's stead. The love and suffering and death of the Son of God all testify to the terrible enormity of sin and declare that there is no escape from its power, no hope of the higher life, but through the submission of the soul to Christ.

The impenitent sometimes excuse themselves by saying of professed Christians, "I am as good as they are. They are no more self-denying, sober, or circumspect in their conduct than I am. They love pleasure and self-indulgence as well as I do." Thus they make the faults of others an excuse for their own neglect of duty. But the sins and defects of others do not excuse anyone, for the Lord has not given us an erring human pattern. The spotless Son of God has been given as our example, and those who complain of the wrong course of professed Christians are the ones who should show better lives and nobler examples. If they have so high a conception of what a Christian should be, is not their own sin so much the greater? They know what is right, and yet refuse to do it.

Beware of procrastination. Do not put off the work of forsaking your sins and seeking purity of heart through Jesus. Here is where thousands upon thousands have erred to their eternal loss. I will not here dwell upon the shortness and uncertainty of life; but there is a terrible danger—a danger not sufficiently understood—in delaying to yield to the pleading voice of God's Holy Spirit, in choosing to live in sin; for such this delay really is. Sin, however small it may be esteemed, can be indulged in only at the peril of infinite loss. What we do not overcome, will overcome us and work out our destruction.

Adam and Eve persuaded themselves that in so small a matter as eating of the forbidden fruit there could not result such terrible consequences as God had declared. But this small matter was the transgression of God's immutable and holy law, and it separated man from God and opened the floodgates of death and untold woe upon our world. Age after age there has gone up from our earth a continual cry of mourning, and the whole creation groaneth and travaileth together in pain as a consequence of man's disobedience. Heaven itself has felt the effects of his rebellion against God. Calvary stands as a memorial of the amazing sacrifice required to atone for the transgression of the divine law. Let us not regard sin as a trivial thing.

Every act of transgression, every neglect or rejection of the grace of Christ, is reacting upon yourself; it is hardening the heart, depraving the will, benumbing the understanding, and not only making you less inclined to yield, but less capable of yielding, to the tender pleading of God's Holy Spirit.

Many are quieting a troubled conscience with the thought that they can change a course of evil when they choose; that they can trifle with the invitations of mercy, and yet be again and again impressed. They think that after doing despite to the Spirit of grace, after casting their influence on the side of Satan, in a moment of terrible extremity they can change their course. But this is not so easily done. The experience, the education, of a lifetime, has so thoroughly molded the character that few then desire to receive the image of Jesus.

Even one wrong trait of character, one sinful desire, persistently cherished, will eventually neutralize all the power of the gospel. Every sinful indulgence strengthens the soul's aversion to God. The man who manifests an infidel hardihood, or a stolid indifference to divine truth, is but reaping the harvest of that which he has himself sown. In all the Bible there is not a more fearful warning against trifling with evil than the words of the wise man that the sinner "shall be holden with the cords of his sins." Proverbs 5:22.

Christ is ready to set us free from sin, but He does not force the will; and if by persistent transgression the will itself is wholly bent on evil, and we do not *desire* to be set free, if we *will* not accept His grace, what more can He do? We have destroyed ourselves by our determined rejection of His love. "Behold, now is the accepted time; behold, now is the day of salvation." "Today if ye will hear His voice, harden not your hearts." 2 Corinthians 6:2; Hebrews 3:7, 8.

"Man looketh on the outward appearance, but the Lord looketh on the heart"—the human heart, with its conflicting emotions of joy and sorrow; the wandering, wayward heart, which is the abode of so much impurity and deceit. 1 Samuel 16:7. He knows its motives, its very intents and purposes. Go to Him with your soul all stained as it is. Like the psalmist, throw its chambers open to the all-seeing eye, exclaiming, "Search me, O God, and know my heart: try me, and know my thoughts: and see if there be any wicked way in me, and lead me in the way everlasting." Psalm 139: 23, 24.

Many accept an intellectual religion, a form of godliness, when the heart is not cleansed. Let it be your prayer, "Create in me a clean heart, O God; and renew a right spirit within me." Psalm 51:10. Deal truly with your own soul. Be as earnest, as persistent, as you would be if your mortal life were at stake. This is a matter to be settled between God and your own soul, settled for eternity. A supposed hope, and nothing more, will prove your ruin.

Study God's word prayerfully. That word presents before you, in the law of God and the life of Christ, the great principles of holiness, without which "no man shall see the Lord." Hebrews 12:14. It convinces of sin; it plainly reveals the way of salvation. Give heed to it as the voice of God speaking to your soul.

As you see the enormity of sin, as you see yourself as you really are, do not give up to despair. It was sinners that Christ came to save. We have not to reconcile God to us, but—O wondrous love!—God in Christ is "reconciling the world unto Himself." 2 Corinthians 5:19. He is wooing by His tender love the hearts of His erring children. No earthly parent could be as patient with the faults and mistakes of his children, as is God with those He seeks to save. No one could plead more tenderly with the transgressor. No human lips ever poured out more tender entreaties to the wanderer than does He. All His promises, His warnings, are but the breathing of unutterable love.

When Satan comes to tell you that you are a great sinner, look up to your Redeemer and talk of His merits. That which will help you is to look to His light. Acknowledge your sin, but tell the enemy that "Christ Jesus came into the world to save sinners" and that you may be saved by His matchless love. 1 Timothy 1:15. Jesus asked Simon a question in regard to two debtors. One owed his lord a small sum, and the other owed him a very large sum; but he forgave them both, and Christ asked Simon which debtor would love his lord most. Simon answered, "He to whom he forgave most." Luke 7:43. We have been great sinners, but Christ died that we might be forgiven. The merits of His sacrifice are sufficient to present to the Father in our behalf. Those to whom He has forgiven most will love Him most, and will stand nearest to His throne to praise Him for His great love and infinite sacrifice. It is when we most fully comprehend the love of God that we best realize the sinfulness of sin. When we see the length of the chain that was let down for us, when we understand something of the infinite sacrifice that Christ has made in our behalf, the heart is melted with tenderness and contrition.

4

Confession

"He that covereth his sins shall not prosper: but whoso confesseth and forsaketh them shall have mercy." Proverbs 28:13.

The conditions of obtaining mercy of God are simple and just and reasonable. The Lord does not require us to do some grievous thing in order that we may have the forgiveness of sin. We need not make long and wearisome pilgrimages, or perform painful penances, to commend our souls to the God of heaven or to expiate our transgression; but he that confesseth and forsaketh his sin shall have mercy.

The apostle says, "Confess your faults one to another, and pray one for another, that ye may be healed." James 5:16. Confess your sins to God, who only can forgive them, and your faults to one another. If you have given offense to your friend or neighbor, you are to acknowledge your wrong, and it is his duty freely to forgive you. Then you are to seek the forgiveness of God, because the brother you have wounded is the property of God, and in injuring him you sinned against his Creator and Redeemer. The case is brought before the only true Mediator, our great High Priest, who "was in all points tempted like as we are, yet without sin," and who is "touched with the feeling of our infirmities," and is able to cleanse from every stain of iniquity. Hebrews 4:15.

Those who have not humbled their souls before God in acknowledging their guilt, have not yet fulfilled the first condition of acceptance. If we have not experienced that repentance which is not to be repented of, and have not with true humiliation of soul and brokenness of spirit confessed our sins, abhorring our iniquity, we have never truly sought for the forgiveness of sin; and if we have never sought, we have never found the peace of God. The only reason why we do not have remission of sins that are past is that we are not willing to humble our hearts and comply with the conditions of the word of truth. Explicit instruction is given concerning this matter. Confession of sin, whether public or private, should be heartfelt and freely expressed. It is not to be urged from the sinner. It is not to be made in a flippant and careless way, or forced from those who have no realizing sense of the abhorrent character of sin. The confession that is the outpouring of the inmost soul finds its way to the God of infinite pity. The psalmist says, "The Lord is nigh unto them that are of a broken heart; and saveth such as be of a contrite spirit." Psalm 34:18.

True confession is always of a specific character, and acknowledges particular sins. They may be of such a nature as to be brought before God only; they may be wrongs that should be confessed to individuals who have suffered injury through them; or they may be of a public character, and should then be as publicly confessed. But all confession should be definite and to the point, acknowledging the very sins of which you are guilty.

In the days of Samuel the Israelites wandered from God. They were suffering the consequences of sin; for they had lost their faith in God, lost their discernment of His power and wisdom to rule the nation, lost their confidence in His ability to defend and vindicate His cause. They turned from the great Ruler of the universe and desired to be governed as were the nations around them. Before they found peace they made this definite confession: "We have added unto all our sins this evil, to ask us a king." 1 Samuel 12:19. The very sin of which they were convicted had to be confessed. Their ingratitude oppressed their souls and severed them from God.

Confession will not be acceptable to God without sincere repentance and reformation. There must be decided changes in the life; everything offensive to God must be put away. This will be the result of genuine sorrow for sin. The work that we have to do on our part is plainly set before us: "Wash you, make you clean; put away the evil of your doings from before Mine eyes; cease to do evil; learn to do well; seek judgment, relieve the oppressed, judge the fatherless, plead for the widow." Isaiah 1:16, 17. "If the wicked restore the pledge, give again that he had robbed, walk in the statutes of life, without committing iniquity; he shall surely live, he shall not die." Ezekiel 33:15. Paul says, speaking of the work of repentance: "Ye sorrowed after a godly sort, what carefulness it wrought in you, yea, what clearing of yourselves, yea, what indignation, yea, what fear, yea, what vehement desire, yea, what zeal, yea, what revenge! In all things ye have approved yourselves to be clear in this matter." 2 Corinthians 7:11.

When sin has deadened the moral perceptions, the wrongdoer does not discern the defects of his character nor realize the enormity of the evil he has committed; and unless he yields to the convicting power of the Holy Spirit he remains in partial blindness to his sin. His confessions are not sincere and in earnest. To every acknowledgment of his guilt he adds an apology in excuse of his course, declaring that if it had not been for certain circumstances he would not have done this or that for which he is reproved.

After Adam and Eve had eaten of the forbidden fruit, they were filled with a sense of shame and terror. At first their only thought was how to excuse their sin and escape the dreaded sentence of death. When the Lord inquired concerning their sin, Adam replied, laying the guilt partly upon God and partly upon his companion: "The woman whom Thou gavest to be with me, she gave me of the tree, and I did eat." The woman put the blame upon the serpent, saying, "The serpent beguiled me, and I did eat." Genesis 3: 12, 13. Why did You make the serpent? Why did You suffer him to come into Eden? These were the questions implied in her excuse for her sin, thus charging God with the responsibility of their fall. The spirit of self-justification originated in the father of lies and has been exhibited by all the sons and daughters of Adam. Confessions of this order are not inspired by the divine Spirit and will not be acceptable to God. True repentance will lead a man to bear his guilt himself and acknowledge it without deception or hypocrisy. Like the poor publican, not lifting up so much as his eyes unto heaven, he will cry, "God be merciful to me a sinner," and those who do acknowledge their guilt will be justified, for Jesus will plead His blood in behalf of the repentant soul.

The examples in God's word of genuine repentance and humiliation reveal a spirit of confession in which there is no excuse for sin or attempt at self-justification. Paul did not seek to shield himself; he paints his sin in its darkest hue, not attempting to lessen his guilt. He says, "Many of the saints did I shut up in prison, having received authority from the chief priests; and when they were put to death, I gave my voice against them. And I punished them oft in every synagogue, and compelled them to blaspheme; and being exceedingly mad against them, I persecuted them even unto strange cities." Acts 26: 10, 11. He does not hesitate to declare that "Christ Jesus came into the world to save sinners; of whom I am chief." 1 Timothy 1:15.

The humble and broken heart, subdued by genuine repentance, will appreciate something of the love of God and the cost of Calvary; and as a son confesses to a loving father, so will the truly penitent bring all his sins before God. And it is written, "If we confess our sins, He is faithful and just to forgive us our sins, and to cleanse us from all unrighteousness." 1 John 1:9.

5

Consecration

God's promise is, "Ye shall seek Me, and find Me, when ye shall search for Me with all your heart." Jeremiah 29:13.

The whole heart must be yielded to God, or the change can never be wrought in us by which we are to be restored to His likeness. By nature we are alienated from God. The Holy Spirit describes our condition in such words as these: "Dead in trespasses and sins;" "the whole head is sick, and the whole heart faint;" "no soundness in it." We are held fast in the snare of Satan, "taken captive by him at his will." Ephesians 2:1; Isaiah 1:5, 6; 2 Timothy 2:26. God desires to heal us, to set us free. But since this requires an entire transformation, a renewing of our whole nature, we must yield ourselves wholly to Him.

The warfare against self is the greatest battle that was ever fought. The yielding of self, surrendering all to the will of God, requires a struggle; but the soul must submit to God before it can be renewed in holiness.

The government of God is not, as Satan would make it appear, founded upon a blind submission, an unreasoning control. It appeals to the intellect and the conscience. "Come now, and let us reason together" is the Creator's invitation to the beings He has made. Isaiah 1:18. God does not force the will of His creatures. He cannot accept an homage that is not willingly and intelligently given. A mere forced submission would prevent all real development of mind or character; it would make man a mere automaton. Such is not the purpose of the Creator. He desires that man, the crowning work of His creative power, shall reach the highest possible development. He sets before us the height of blessing to which He desires to bring us through His grace. He invites us to give ourselves to Him, that He may work His will in us. It remains for us to choose whether we will be set free from the bondage of sin, to share the glorious liberty of the sons of God.

In giving ourselves to God, we must necessarily give up all that would separate us from Him. Hence the Saviour says, "Whosoever he be of you that forsaketh not all that he hath, he cannot be My disciple." Luke 14:33. Whatever shall draw away the heart from God must be given up. Mammon is the idol of many. The love of money, the desire for wealth, is the golden chain that binds them to Satan. Reputation and worldly honor are worshiped by another class. The life of selfish ease and freedom from responsibility is the idol of others. But these slavish bands must be broken. We cannot be half the Lord's and half the world's. We are not God's children unless we are such entirely.

There are those who profess to serve God, while they rely upon their own efforts to obey His law, to form a right character, and secure salvation. Their hearts are not moved by any deep sense of the love of Christ, but they seek to perform the duties of the Christian life as that which God requires of them in order to gain heaven. Such religion is worth nothing. When Christ dwells in the heart, the soul will be so filled with His love, with the joy of communion with Him, that it will cleave to Him; and in the contemplation of Him, self will be forgotten. Love to Christ will be the spring of action. Those who feel the constraining love of God, do not ask how little may be given to meet the requirements of God; they do not ask for the lowest standard, but aim at perfect conformity to the will of their Redeemer. With earnest desire they yield all and manifest an interest proportionate to the value of the object which they seek. A profession of Christ without this deep love is mere talk, dry formality, and heavy drudgery.

Do you feel that it is too great a sacrifice to yield all to Christ? Ask yourself the question, "What has Christ given for me?" The Son of God gave all—life and love and suffering—for our redemption. And can it be that we, the unworthy objects of so great love, will withhold our hearts from Him? Every moment of our lives we have been partakers of the blessings of His grace, and for this very reason we cannot fully realize the depths of ignorance and misery from which we have been saved. Can we look upon Him whom our sins have pierced, and yet be willing to do despite to all His love and sacrifice? In view of the infinite humiliation of the Lord of glory, shall we murmur because we can enter into life only through conflict and self-abasement?

The inquiry of many a proud heart is, "Why need I go in penitence and humiliation before I can have the assurance of my acceptance with God?" I point you to Christ. He was sinless, and, more than this, He was the Prince of heaven; but in man's behalf He became sin for the race. "He was numbered with the transgressors; and He bare the sin of many, and made intercession for the transgressors." Isaiah 53:12.

But what do we give up, when we give all? A sin-polluted heart, for Jesus to purify, to cleanse by His own blood, and to save by His matchless love. And yet men think it hard to give up all! I am ashamed to hear it spoken of, ashamed to write it.

God does not require us to give up anything that it is for our best interest to retain. In all that He does, He has the well-being of His children in view. Would that all who have not chosen Christ might realize that He has something vastly better to offer them than they are seeking for themselves. Man is doing the greatest injury and injustice to his own soul when he thinks and acts contrary to the will of God. No real joy can be found in the path forbidden by Him who knows what is best and who plans for the good of His creatures. The path of transgression is the path of misery and destruction.

It is a mistake to entertain the thought that God is pleased to see His children suffer. All heaven is interested in the happiness of man. Our heavenly Father does not close the avenues of joy to any of His creatures. The divine requirements call upon us to shun those indulgences that would bring suffering and disappointment, that would close to us the door of happiness and heaven.

The world's Redeemer accepts men as they are, with all their wants, imperfections, and weaknesses; and He will not only cleanse from sin and grant redemption through His blood, but will satisfy the heart-longing of all who consent to wear His yoke, to bear His burden. It is His purpose to impart peace and rest to all who come to Him for the bread of life. He requires us to perform only those duties that will lead our steps to heights of bliss to which the disobedient can never attain. The true, joyous life of the soul is to have Christ formed within, the hope of glory.

Many are inquiring, "*How* am I to make the surrender of myself to God?" You desire to give yourself to Him, but you are weak in moral power, in slavery to doubt, and controlled by the habits of your life of sin. Your promises and resolutions are like ropes of sand. You cannot control your thoughts, your impulses, your affections. The knowledge of your broken promises and forfeited pledges weakens your confidence in your own sincerity, and causes you to feel that God cannot accept you; but you need not despair. What you need to understand is the true force of the will. This is the governing power in the nature of man, the power of decision, or of choice. Everything depends on the right action of the will. The power of choice God has given to men; it is theirs to exercise. You cannot change your heart, you cannot of yourself give to God its affections; but you can *choose* to serve Him. You can give Him your will; He will then work in you to will and to do according to His good pleasure. Thus your whole nature will be brought under the control of the Spirit of Christ; your affections will be centered upon Him, your thoughts will be in harmony with Him.

Desires for goodness and holiness are right as far as they go; but if you stop here, they will avail nothing. Many will be lost while hoping and desiring to be Christians. They do not come to the point of yielding the will to God. They do not now *choose* to be Christians.

Through the right exercise of the will, an entire change may be made in your life. By yielding up your will to Christ, you ally yourself with the power that is above all principalities and powers. You will have strength from above to hold you steadfast, and thus through constant surrender to God you will be enabled to live the new life, even the life of faith.

6

Faith and Acceptance

As your conscience has been quickened by the Holy Spirit, you have seen something of the evil of sin, of its power, its guilt, its woe; and you look upon it with abhorrence. You feel that sin has separated you from God, that you are in bondage to the power of evil. The more you struggle to escape, the more you realize your helplessness. Your motives are impure; your heart is unclean. You see that your life has been filled with selfishness and sin. You long to be forgiven, to be cleansed, to be set free. Harmony with God, likeness to Him—what can you do to obtain it?

It is peace that you need—Heaven's forgiveness and peace and love in the soul. Money cannot buy it, intellect cannot procure it, wisdom cannot attain to it; you can never hope, by your own efforts, to secure it. But God offers it to you as a gift, "without money and without price." Isaiah 55:1. It is yours if you will but reach out your hand and grasp it. The Lord says, "Though your sins be as scarlet, they shall be as white as snow; though they be red like crimson, they shall be as wool." Isaiah 1:18. "A new heart also will I give you, and a new spirit will I put within you." Ezekiel 36:26.

You have confessed your sins, and in heart put them away. You have resolved to give yourself to God. Now go to Him, and ask that He will wash away your sins and give you a new heart. Then believe that He does this *because He has promised*. This is the lesson which Jesus taught while He was on earth, that the gift which God promises us, we must believe we do receive, and it is ours. Jesus healed the people of their diseases when they had faith in His power; He helped them in the things which they could see, thus inspiring them with confidence in Him concerning things which they could not see—leading them to believe in His power to forgive sins. This He plainly stated in the healing of the man sick with palsy: *"That ye may know that the Son of man hath power on earth to forgive sins*, (then saith He to the sick of the palsy,) Arise, take up thy bed, and go unto thine house." Matthew 9:6. So also John the evangelist says, speaking of the miracles of Christ, "These are written, that ye might believe that Jesus is the Christ, the Son of God; and that believing ye might have life through His name." John 20:31.

From the simple Bible account of how Jesus healed the sick, we may learn something about how to believe in Him for the forgiveness of sins. Let us turn to the story of the paralytic at Bethesda. The poor sufferer was helpless; he had not used his limbs for thirty-eight years. Yet Jesus bade him, "Rise, take up thy bed, and walk." The sick man might have said, "Lord, if Thou wilt make me whole, I will obey Thy word." But, no, he believed Christ's word, believed that he was made whole, and he made the effort at once; he *willed* to walk, and he did walk. He acted on the word of Christ, and God gave the power. He was made whole.

In like manner you are a sinner. You cannot atone for your past sins; you cannot change your heart and make yourself holy. But God promises to do all this for you through Christ. You *believe* that promise. You confess your sins and give yourself to God. You *will* to serve Him. Just as surely as you do this, God will fulfill His word to you. If you believe the promise,—believe that you are forgiven and cleansed,—God supplies the fact; you are made whole, just as Christ gave the paralytic power to walk when the man believed that he was healed. It *is* so if you believe it.

Do not wait to *feel* that you are made whole, but say, "I believe it; it *is* so, not because I feel it, but because God has promised."

Jesus says, "What things soever ye desire, when ye pray, believe that ye receive them, and ye shall have them." Mark 11:24. There is a condition to this promise—that we pray according to the will of God. But it is the will of God to cleanse us from sin, to make us His children, and to enable us to live a holy life. So we may ask for these blessings, and believe that we receive them, and thank God that we *have* received them. It is our privilege to go to Jesus and be cleansed, and to stand before the law without shame or remorse. "There is therefore now no condemnation to them which are in Christ Jesus, who walk not after the flesh, but after the Spirit." Romans 8:1.

Henceforth you are not your own; you are bought with a price. "Ye were not redeemed with corruptible things, as silver and gold; . . . but with the precious blood of Christ, as of a lamb without blemish and without spot." 1 Peter 1:18, 19. Through this simple act of believing God, the Holy Spirit has begotten a new life in your heart. You are as a child born into the family of God, and He loves you as He loves His Son.

Now that you have given yourself to Jesus, do not draw back, do not take yourself away from Him, but day by day say, "I am Christ's; I have given myself to Him;" and ask Him to give you His Spirit and keep you by His grace. As it is by giving yourself to God, and believing Him, that you become His child, so you are to live in Him. The apostle says, "As ye have therefore received Christ Jesus the Lord, so walk ye in Him." Colossians 2:6.

Some seem to feel that they must be on probation, and must prove to the Lord that they are reformed, before they can claim His blessing. But they may claim the blessing of God even now. They must have His grace, the Spirit of Christ, to help their infirmities, or they cannot resist evil. Jesus loves to have us come to Him just as we are, sinful, helpless, dependent. We may come with all our weakness, our folly, our sinfulness, and fall at His feet in penitence. It is His glory to encircle us in the arms of His love and to bind up our wounds, to cleanse us from all impurity.

Here is where thousands fail; they do not believe that Jesus pardons them personally, individually. They do not take God at His word. It is the privilege of all who comply with the conditions to know for themselves that pardon is freely extended for every sin. Put away the suspicion that God's promises are not meant for you. They are for every repentant transgressor. Strength and grace have been provided through Christ to be brought by ministering angels to every believing soul. None are so sinful that they cannot find strength, purity, and righteousness in Jesus, who died for them. He is waiting to strip them of their garments stained and polluted with sin, and to put upon them the white robes of righteousness; He bids them live and not die.

God does not deal with us as finite men deal with one another. His thoughts are thoughts of mercy, love, and tenderest compassion. He says, "Let the wicked forsake his way, and the unrighteous man his thoughts: and let him return unto the Lord, and He will have mercy upon him; and to our God, for He will abundantly pardon." "I have blotted out, as a thick cloud, thy transgressions, and, as a cloud, thy sins." Isaiah 55:7; 44:22.

"I have no pleasure in the death of him that dieth, saith the Lord God: wherefore turn yourselves, and live ye." Ezekiel 18:32. Satan is ready to steal away the blessed assurances of God. He desires to take every glimmer of hope and every ray of light from the soul; but you must not permit him to do this. Do not give ear to the tempter, but say, "Jesus has died that I might live. He loves me, and wills not that I should perish. I have a compassionate heavenly Father; and although I have abused His love, though the blessings He has given me have been squandered, I will arise, and go to my Father, and say, 'I have sinned against heaven, and before Thee, and am no more worthy to be called Thy son: make me as one of Thy hired servants.' " The parable tells you how the wanderer will be received: "*When he was yet a great way off,* his father saw him, and had compassion, and ran, and fell on his neck, and kissed him." Luke 15:18-20.

But even this parable, tender and touching as it is, comes short of expressing the infinite compassion of the heavenly Father. The Lord declares by His prophet, "I have loved thee with an everlasting love: *therefore with loving-kindness have I drawn thee.*" Jeremiah 31:3. While the sinner is yet far from the Father's house, wasting his substance in a strange country, the Father's heart is yearning over him; and every longing awakened in the soul to return to God is but the tender pleading of His Spirit, wooing, entreating, drawing the wanderer to his Father's heart of love.

With the rich promises of the Bible before you, can you give place to doubt? Can you believe that when the poor sinner longs to return, longs to forsake his sins, the Lord sternly withholds him from coming to His feet in repentance? Away with such thoughts! Nothing can hurt your own soul more than to entertain such a conception of our heavenly Father. He hates sin, but He loves the sinner, and He gave Himself in the person of Christ, that all who would might be saved and have eternal blessedness in the kingdom of glory. What stronger or more tender language could have been employed than He has chosen in which to express His love toward us? He declares, "Can a woman forget her sucking child, that she should not have compassion on the son of her womb? yea, they may forget, yet will I not forget thee." Isaiah 49:15.

Look up, you that are doubting and trembling; for Jesus lives to make intercession for us. Thank God for the gift of His dear Son and pray that He may not have died for you in vain. The Spirit invites you today. Come with your whole heart to Jesus, and you may claim His blessing.

As you read the promises, remember they are the expression of unutterable love and pity. The great heart of Infinite Love is drawn toward the sinner with boundless compassion. "We have redemption through His blood, the forgiveness of sins." Ephesians 1:7. Yes, only believe that God is your helper. He wants to restore His moral image in man. As you draw near to Him with confession and repentance, He will draw near to you with mercy and forgiveness.

7

The Test of Discipleship

"If any man be in Christ, he is a new creature: old things are passed away; behold, all things are become new." 2 Corinthians 5:17.

A person may not be able to tell the exact time or place, or trace all the chain of circumstances in the process of conversion; but this does not prove him to be unconverted. Christ said to Nicodemus, "The wind bloweth where it listeth, and thou hearest the sound thereof, but canst not tell whence it cometh, and whither it goeth: so is everyone that is born of the Spirit." John 3:8. Like the wind, which is invisible, yet the effects of which are plainly seen and felt, is the Spirit of God in its work upon the human heart. That regenerating power, which no human eye can see, begets a new life in the soul; it creates a new being in the image of God. While the work of the Spirit is silent and imperceptible, its effects are manifest. If the heart has been renewed by the Spirit of God, the life will bear witness to the fact. While we cannot do anything to change our hearts or to bring ourselves into harmony with God; while we must not trust at all to ourselves or our good works, our lives will reveal whether the grace of God is dwelling within us. A change will be seen in the character, the habits, the pursuits. The contrast will be clear and decided between what they have been and what they are. The character is revealed, not by occasional good deeds and occasional misdeeds, but by the tendency of the habitual words and acts.

It is true that there may be an outward correctness of deportment without the renewing power of Christ. The love of influence and the desire for the esteem of others may produce a well-ordered life. Self-respect may lead us to avoid the appearance of evil. A selfish heart may perform generous actions. By what means, then, shall we determine whose side we are on?

Who has the heart? With whom are our thoughts? Of whom do we love to converse? Who has our warmest affections and our best energies? If we are Christ's, our thoughts are with Him, and our sweetest thoughts are of Him. All we have and are is consecrated to Him. We long to bear His image, breathe His spirit, do His will, and please Him in all things.

Those who become new creatures in Christ Jesus will bring forth the fruits of the Spirit, "love, joy, peace, long-suffering, gentleness, goodness, faith, meekness, temperance." Galatians 5:22, 23. They will no longer fashion themselves according to the former lusts, but by the faith of the Son of God they will follow in His steps, reflect His character, and purify themselves even as He is pure. The things they once hated they now love, and the things they once loved they hate. The proud and self-assertive become meek and lowly in heart. The vain and supercilious become serious and unobtrusive. The drunken become sober, and the profligate pure. The vain customs and fashions of the world are laid aside. Christians will seek not the "outward adorning," but "the hidden man of the heart, in that which is not corruptible, even the ornament of a meek and quiet spirit." 1 Peter 3: 3, 4.

There is no evidence of genuine repentance unless it works reformation. If he restore the pledge, give again that he had robbed, confess his sins, and love God and his fellow men, the sinner may be sure that he has passed from death unto life.

When, as erring, sinful beings, we come to Christ and become partakers of His pardoning grace, love springs up in the heart. Every burden is light, for the yoke that Christ imposes is easy. Duty becomes a delight, and sacrifice a pleasure. The path that before seemed shrouded in darkness, becomes bright with beams from the Sun of Righteousness.

The loveliness of the character of Christ will be seen in His followers. It was His delight to do the will of God. Love to God, zeal for His glory, was the controlling power in our Saviour's life. Love beautified and ennobled all His actions. Love is of God. The unconsecrated heart cannot originate or produce it. It is found only in the heart where Jesus reigns. "We love, because He first loved us." 1 John 4:19, R.V. In the heart renewed by divine grace, love is the principle of action. It modifies the character, governs the impulses, controls the passions, subdues enmity, and ennobles the affections. This love, cherished in the soul, sweetens the life and sheds a refining influence on all around.

There are two errors against which the children of God—particularly those who have just come to trust in His grace—especially need to guard. The first, already dwelt upon, is that of looking to their own works, trusting to anything they can do, to bring themselves into harmony with God. He who is trying to become holy by his own works in keeping the law, is attempting an impossibility. All that man can do without Christ is polluted with selfishness and sin. It is the grace of Christ alone, through faith, that can make us holy.

The opposite and no less dangerous error is that belief in Christ releases men from keeping the law of God; that since by faith alone we become partakers of the grace of Christ, our works have nothing to do with our redemption.

But notice here that obedience is not a mere outward compliance, but the service of love. The law of God is an expression of His very nature; it is an embodiment of the great principle of love, and hence is the foundation of His government in heaven and earth. If our hearts are renewed in the likeness of God, if the divine love is implanted in the soul, will not the law of God be carried out in the life? When the principle of love is implanted in the heart, when man is renewed after the image of Him that created him, the new-covenant promise is fulfilled, "I will put My laws into their hearts, and in their minds will I write them." Hebrews 10:16. And if the law is written in the heart, will it not shape the life? Obedience—the service and allegiance of love—is the true sign of discipleship. Thus the Scripture says, "This is the love of God, that we keep His commandments." "He that saith, I know Him, and keepeth not His commandments, is a liar, and the truth is not in him." 1 John 5:3; 2:4.

Instead of releasing man from obedience, it is faith, and faith only, that makes us partakers of the grace of Christ, which enables us to render obedience.

We do not earn salvation by our obedience; for salvation is the free gift of God, to be received by faith. But obedience is the fruit of faith. "Ye know that He was manifested to take away our sins; and in Him is no sin. Whosoever abideth in Him sinneth not: whosoever sinneth hath not seen Him, neither known Him." 1 John 3:5, 6. Here is the true test. If we abide in Christ, if the love of God dwells in us, our feelings, our thoughts, our purposes, our actions, will be in harmony with the will of God as expressed in the precepts of His holy law. "Little children, let no man deceive you: he that doeth righteousness is righteous, even as He is righteous." 1 John 3:7. Righteousness is defined by the standard of God's holy law, as expressed in the ten precepts given on Sinai.

That so-called faith in Christ which professes to release men from the obligation of obedience to God, is not faith, but presumption. "By grace are ye saved through faith." But "faith, if it hath not works, is dead." Ephesians 2:8; James 2:17. Jesus said of Himself before He came to earth, "I delight to do Thy will, O My God: yea, Thy law is within My heart." Psalm 40:8. And just before He ascended again to heaven He declared, "I have kept My Father's commandments, and abide in His love." John 15:10. The Scripture says, "Hereby we do know that we know Him, if we keep His commandments. . . . He that saith he abideth in Him ought himself also so to walk even as He walked." 1 John 2:3-6. "Because Christ also suffered for us, leaving us an example, that ye should follow His steps." 1 Peter 2:21.

The condition of eternal life is now just what it always has been,—just what it was in Paradise before the fall of our first parents,—perfect obedience to the law of God, perfect righteousness. If eternal life were granted on any condition short of this, then the happiness of the whole universe would be imperiled. The way would be open for sin, with all its train of woe and misery, to be immortalized.

It was possible for Adam, before the fall, to form a righteous character by obedience to God's law. But he failed to do this, and because of his sin our natures are fallen and we cannot make ourselves righteous. Since we are sinful, unholy, we cannot perfectly obey the holy law. We have no righteousness of our own with which to meet the claims of the law of God. But Christ has made a way of escape for us. He lived on earth amid trials and temptations such as we have to meet. He lived a sinless life. He died for us, and now He offers to take our sins and give us His righteousness. If you give yourself to Him, and accept Him as your Saviour, then, sinful as your life may have been, for His sake you are accounted righteous. Christ's character stands in place of your character, and you are accepted before God just as if you had not sinned.

More than this, Christ changes the heart. He abides in your heart by faith. You are to maintain this connection with Christ by faith and the continual surrender of your will to Him; and so long as you do this, He will work in you to will and to do according to His good pleasure. So you may say, "The life which I now live in the flesh I live by the faith of the Son of God, who loved me, and gave Himself for me." Galatians 2:20. So Jesus said to His disciples, "It is not ye that speak, but the Spirit of your Father which speaketh in you." Matthew 10:20. Then with Christ working in you, you will manifest the same spirit and do the same good works—works of righteousness, obedience.

So we have nothing in ourselves of which to boast. We have no ground for self-exaltation. Our only ground of hope is in the righteousness of Christ imputed to us, and in that wrought by His Spirit working in and through us.

When we speak of faith, there is a distinction that should be borne in mind. There is a kind of belief that is wholly distinct from faith. The existence and power of God, the truth of His word, are facts that even Satan and his hosts cannot at heart deny. The Bible says that "the devils also believe, and tremble;" but this is not faith. James 2:19. Where there is not only a belief in God's word, but a submission of the will to Him; where the heart is yielded to Him, the affections fixed upon Him, there is faith—faith that works by love and purifies the soul. Through this faith the heart is renewed in the image of God. And the heart that in its unrenewed state is not subject to the law of God, neither indeed can be, now delights in its holy precepts, exclaiming with the psalmist, "O how love I Thy law! it is my meditation all the day." Psalm 119:97. And the righteousness of the law is fulfilled in us, "who walk not after the flesh, but after the Spirit." Romans 8:1.

There are those who have known the pardoning love of Christ and who really desire to be children of God, yet they realize that their character is imperfect, their life faulty, and they are ready to doubt whether their hearts have been renewed by the Holy Spirit. To such I would say, Do not draw back in despair. We shall often have to bow down and weep at the feet of Jesus because of our shortcomings and mistakes, but we are not to be discouraged. Even if we are overcome by the enemy, we are not cast off, not forsaken and rejected of God. No; Christ is at the right hand of God, who also maketh intercession for us. Said the beloved John, "These things write I unto you, that ye sin not. And if any man sin, we have an advocate with the Father, Jesus Christ the righteous." 1 John 2:1. And do not forget the words of Christ, "The Father Himself loveth you." John 16:27. He desires to restore you to Himself, to see His own purity and holiness reflected in you. And if you will but yield yourself to Him, He that hath begun a good work in you will carry it forward to the day of Jesus Christ. Pray more fervently; believe more fully. As we come to distrust our own power, let us trust the power of our Redeemer, and we shall praise Him who is the health of our countenance.

The closer you come to Jesus, the more faulty you will appear in your own eyes; for your vision will be clearer, and your imperfections will be seen in broad and distinct contrast to His perfect nature. This is evidence that Satan's delusions have lost their power; that the vivifying influence of the Spirit of God is arousing you.

No deep-seated love for Jesus can dwell in the heart that does not realize its own sinfulness. The soul that is transformed by the grace of Christ will admire His divine character; but if we do not see our own moral deformity, it is unmistakable evidence that we have not had a view of the beauty and excellence of Christ.

The less we see to esteem in ourselves, the more we shall see to esteem in the infinite purity and loveliness of our Saviour. A view of our sinfulness drives us to Him who can pardon; and when the soul, realizing its helplessness, reaches out after Christ, He will reveal Himself in power. The more our sense of need drives us to Him and to the word of God, the more exalted views we shall have of His character, and the more fully we shall reflect His image.

8

Growing Up Into Christ

The change of heart by which we become children of God is in the Bible spoken of as birth. Again, it is compared to the germination of the good seed sown by the husbandman. In like manner those who are just converted to Christ are, "as new-born babes," to "grow up" to the stature of men and women in Christ Jesus. 1 Peter 2:2; Ephesians 4:15. Or like the good seed sown in the field, they are to grow up and bring forth fruit. Isaiah says that they shall "be called trees of righteousness, the planting of the Lord, that He might be glorified." Isaiah 61:3. So from natural life, illustrations are drawn, to help us better to understand the mysterious truths of spiritual life.

Not all the wisdom and skill of man can produce life in the smallest object in nature. It is only through the life which God Himself has imparted, that either plant or animal can live. So it is only through the life from God that spiritual life is begotten in the hearts of men. Unless a man is "born from above," he cannot become a partaker of the life which Christ came to give. John 3:3, margin.

As with life, so it is with growth. It is God who brings the bud to bloom and the flower to fruit. It is by His power that the seed develops, "first the blade, then the ear, after that the full corn in the ear." Mark 4:28. And the prophet Hosea says of Israel, that "he shall grow as the lily." "They shall revive as the corn, and grow as the vine." Hosea 14:5, 7. And Jesus bids us "consider the lilies how they grow." Luke 12:27. The plants and flowers grow not by their own care or anxiety or effort, but by receiving that which God has furnished to minister to their life. The child cannot, by any anxiety or power of its own, add to its stature. No more can you, by anxiety or effort of yourself, secure spiritual growth. The plant, the child, grows by receiving from its surroundings that which ministers to its life—air, sunshine, and food. What these gifts of nature are to animal and plant, such is Christ to those who trust in Him. He is their "everlasting light," "a sun and shield." Isaiah 60:19; Psalm 84:11. He shall be as "the dew unto Israel." "He shall come down like rain upon the mown grass." Hosea 14:5; Psalm 72:6. He is the living water, "the Bread of God . . . which cometh down from heaven, and giveth life unto the world." John 6:33.

In the matchless gift of His Son, God has encircled the whole world with an atmosphere of grace as real as the air which circulates around the globe. All who choose to breathe this life-giving atmosphere will live and grow up to the stature of men and women in Christ Jesus.

As the flower turns to the sun, that the bright beams may aid in perfecting its beauty and symmetry, so should we turn to the Sun of Righteousness, that heaven's light may shine upon us, that our character may be developed into the likeness of Christ.

Jesus teaches the same thing when He says, "Abide in Me, and I in you. As the branch cannot bear fruit of itself, except it abide in the vine; no more can ye, except ye abide in Me. . . . Without Me ye can do nothing." John 15:4, 5. You are just as dependent upon Christ, in order to live a holy life, as is the branch upon the parent stock for growth and fruitfulness. Apart from Him you have no life. You have no power to resist temptation or to grow in grace and holiness. Abiding in Him, you may flourish. Drawing your life from Him, you will not wither nor be fruitless. You will be like a tree planted by the rivers of water.

Many have an idea that they must do some part of the work alone. They have trusted in Christ for the forgiveness of sin, but now they seek by their own efforts to live aright. But every such effort must fail. Jesus says, "Without Me ye can do nothing." Our growth in grace, our joy, our usefulness,—all depend upon our union with Christ. It is by communion with Him, daily, hourly,—by abiding in Him,—that we are to grow in grace. He is not only the Author, but the Finisher of our faith. It is Christ first and last and always. He is to be with us, not only at the beginning and the end of our course, but at every step of the way. David says, "I have set the Lord always before me: because He is at my right hand, I shall not be moved." Psalm 16:8.

Do you ask, "How am I to abide in Christ?" In the same way as you received Him at first. "As ye have therefore received Christ Jesus the Lord, so walk ye in Him." "The just shall live by faith." Colossians 2:6; Hebrews 10:38. You gave yourself to God, to be His wholly, to serve and obey Him, and you took Christ as your Saviour. You could not yourself atone for your sins or change your heart; but having given yourself to God, you believe that He for Christ's sake did all this for you. By *faith* you became Christ's, and by faith you are to grow up in Him—by giving and taking. You are to *give* all,—your heart, your will, your service,—give yourself to Him to obey all His require-ments; and you must *take* all,—Christ, the fullness of all blessing, to abide in your heart, to be your strength, your righteousness, your everlasting helper,—to give you power to obey.

Consecrate yourself to God in the morning; make this your very first work. Let your prayer be, "Take me, O Lord, as wholly Thine. I lay all my plans at Thy feet. Use me today in Thy service. Abide with me, and let all my work be wrought in Thee." This is a daily matter. Each morning consecrate yourself to God for that day. Surrender all your plans to Him, to be carried out or given up as His providence shall indicate. Thus day by day you may be giving your life into the hands of God, and thus your life will be molded more and more after the life of Christ.

A life in Christ is a life of restfulness. There may be no ecstasy of feeling, but there should be an abiding, peaceful trust. Your hope is not in yourself; it is in Christ. Your weakness is united to His strength, your ignorance to His wisdom, your frailty to His enduring might. So you are not to look to yourself, not to let the mind dwell upon self, but look to Christ. Let the mind dwell upon His love, upon the beauty, the perfection, of His character. Christ in His self-denial, Christ in His humiliation, Christ in His purity and holiness, Christ in His matchless love—this is the subject for the soul's contemplation. It is by loving Him, copying Him, depending wholly upon Him, that you are to be transformed into His likeness.

Jesus says, "Abide in Me." These words convey the idea of rest, stability, confidence. Again He invites, "Come unto Me, . . . and I will give you rest." Matthew 11:28. The words of the psalmist express the same thought: "Rest in the Lord, and wait patiently for Him." And Isaiah gives the assurance, "In quietness and in confidence shall be your strength." Psalm 37:7; Isaiah 30:15. This rest is not found in inactivity; for in the Saviour's invitation the promise of rest is united with the call to labor: "Take My yoke upon you: . . . and ye shall find rest." Matthew 11:29. The heart that rests most fully upon Christ will be most earnest and active in labor for Him.

When the mind dwells upon self, it is turned away from Christ, the source of strength and life. Hence it is Satan's constant effort to keep the attention diverted from the Saviour and thus prevent the union and communion of the soul with Christ. The pleasures of the world, life's cares and perplexities and sorrows, the faults of others, or your own faults and imperfections—to any or all of these he will seek to divert the mind. Do not be misled by his devices. Many who are really conscientious, and who desire to live for God, he too often leads to dwell upon their own faults and weaknesses, and thus by separating them from Christ he hopes to gain the victory. We should not make self the center and indulge anxiety and fear as to whether we shall be saved. All this turns the soul away from the Source of our strength. Commit the keeping of your soul to God, and trust in Him. Talk and think of Jesus. Let self be lost in Him. Put away all doubt; dismiss your fears. Say with the apostle Paul, "I live; yet not I, but Christ liveth in me: and the life which I now live in the flesh I live by the faith of the Son of God, who loved me, and gave Himself for me." Galatians 2:20. Rest in God. He is able to keep that which you have committed to Him. If you will leave yourself in His hands, He will bring you off more than conqueror through Him that has loved you.

When Christ took human nature upon Him, He bound humanity to Himself by a tie of love that can never be broken by any power save the choice of man himself. Satan will constantly present allurements to induce us to break this tie—to choose to separate ourselves from Christ. Here is where we need to watch, to strive, to pray, that nothing may entice us to *choose* another master; for we are always free to do this. But let us keep our eyes fixed upon Christ, and He will preserve us. Looking unto Jesus, we are safe. Nothing can pluck us out of His hand. In constantly beholding Him, we "are changed into the same image from glory to glory, even as by the Spirit of the Lord." 2 Corinthians 3:18.

It was thus that the early disciples gained their likeness to the dear Saviour.

When those disciples heard the words of Jesus, they felt their need of Him. They sought, they found, they followed Him. They were with Him in the house, at the table, in the closet, in the field. They were with Him as pupils with a teacher, daily receiving from His lips lessons of holy truth. They looked to Him, as servants to their master, to learn their duty. Those disciples were men "subject to like passions as we are." James 5:17. They had the same battle with sin to fight. They needed the same grace, in order to live a holy life.

Even John, the beloved disciple, the one who most fully reflected the likeness of the Saviour, did not naturally possess that loveliness of character. He was not only self-assertive and ambitious for honor, but impetuous, and resentful under injuries. But as the character of the Divine One was manifested to him, he saw his own deficiency and was humbled by the knowledge. The strength and patience, the power and tenderness, the majesty and meekness, that he beheld in the daily life of the Son of God, filled his soul with admiration and love. Day by day his heart was drawn out toward Christ, until he lost sight of self in love for his Master. His resentful, ambitious temper was yielded to the molding power of Christ. The regenerating influence of the Holy Spirit renewed his heart. The power of the love of Christ wrought a transformation of character. This is the sure result of union with Jesus. When Christ abides in the heart, the whole nature is transformed. Christ's Spirit, His love, softens the heart, subdues the soul, and raises the thoughts and desires toward God and heaven.

When Christ ascended to heaven, the sense of His presence was still with His followers. It was a personal presence, full of love and light. Jesus, the Saviour, who had walked and talked and prayed with them, who had spoken hope and comfort to their hearts, had, while the message of peace was still upon His lips, been taken up from them into heaven, and the tones of His voice had come back to them, as the cloud of angels received Him—"Lo, I am with you alway, even unto the end of the world." Matthew 28:20. He had ascended to heaven in the form of humanity. They knew that He was before the throne of God, their Friend and Saviour still; that His sympathies were unchanged; that He was still identified with suffering humanity. He was presenting before God the merits of His own precious blood, showing His wounded hands and feet, in remembrance of the price He had paid for His redeemed. They knew that He had ascended to heaven to prepare places for them, and that He would come again and take them to Himself.

As they met together after the ascension they were eager to present their requests to the Father in the name of Jesus. In solemn awe they bowed in prayer, repeating the assurance, "Whatsoever ye shall ask the Father in My name, He will give it you. Hitherto have ye asked nothing in My name: ask, and ye shall receive, that your joy may be full." John 16:23, 24. They extended the hand of faith higher and higher with the mighty argument, "It is Christ that died, yea rather, that is risen again, who is even at the right hand of God, who also maketh intercession for us." Romans 8:34. And Pentecost brought them the presence of the Comforter, of whom Christ had said, He "shall be in you." And He had further said, "It is expedient for you that I go away: for if I go not away, the Comforter will not come unto you; but if I depart, I will send Him unto you." John 14:17; 16:7. Henceforth through the Spirit, Christ was to abide continually in the hearts of His children. Their union with Him was closer than when He was personally with them. The light, and love, and power of the indwelling Christ shone out through them, so that men, beholding, "marveled; and they took knowledge of them, that they had been with Jesus." Acts 4:13.

All that Christ was to the disciples, He desires to be to His children today; for in that last prayer, with the little band of disciples gathered about Him, He said, "Neither pray I for these alone, but for them also which shall believe on Me through their word." John 17:20.

Jesus prayed for us, and He asked that we might be one with Him, even as He is one with the Father. What a union is this! The Saviour has said of Himself, "The Son can do nothing of Himself;" "the Father that dwelleth in Me, He doeth the works." John 5:19; 14:10. Then if Christ is dwelling in our hearts, He will work in us "both to will and to do of His good pleasure." Philippians 2:13. We shall work as He worked; we shall manifest the same spirit. And thus, loving Him and abiding in Him, we shall "grow up into Him in all things, which is the head, even Christ." Ephesians 4:15.

9

The Work and the Life

God is the source of life and light and joy to the universe. Like rays of light from the sun, like the streams of water bursting from a living spring, blessings flow out from Him to all His creatures. And wherever the life of God is in the hearts of men, it will flow out to others in love and blessing.

Our Saviour's joy was in the uplifting and redemption of fallen men. For this He counted not His life dear unto Himself, but endured the cross, despising the shame. So angels are ever engaged in working for the happiness of others. This is their joy. That which selfish hearts would regard as humiliating service, ministering to those who are wretched and in every way inferior in character and rank, is the work of sinless angels. The spirit of Christ's self-sacrificing love is the spirit that pervades heaven and is the very essence of its bliss. This is the spirit that Christ's followers will possess, the work that they will do.

When the love of Christ is enshrined in the heart, like sweet fragrance it cannot be hidden. Its holy influence will be felt by all with whom we come in contact. The spirit of Christ in the heart is like a spring in the desert, flowing to refresh all and making those who are ready to perish, eager to drink of the water of life.

Love to Jesus will be manifested in a desire to work as He worked for the blessing and uplifting of humanity. It will lead to love, tenderness, and sympathy toward all the creatures of our heavenly Father's care.

The Saviour's life on earth was not a life of ease and devotion to Himself, but He toiled with persistent, earnest, untiring effort for the salvation of lost mankind. From the manger to Calvary He followed the path of self-denial and sought not to be released from arduous tasks, painful travels and exhausting care and labor. He said, "The Son of man came not to be ministered unto, but to minister, and to give His life a ransom for many." Matthew 20:28. This was the one great object of His life. Everything else was secondary and subservient. It was His meat and drink to do the will of God and to finish His work. Self and self-interest had no part in His labor.

So those who are the partakers of the grace of Christ will be ready to make any sacrifice, that others for whom He died may share the heavenly gift. They will do all they can to make the world better for their stay in it. This spirit is the sure outgrowth of a soul truly converted. No sooner does one come to Christ than there is born in his heart a desire to make known to others what a precious friend he has found in Jesus; the saving and sanctifying truth cannot be shut up in his heart. If we are clothed with the righteousness of Christ and are filled with the joy of His indwelling Spirit, we shall not be able to hold our peace. If we have tasted and seen that the Lord is good we shall have something to tell. Like Philip when he found the Saviour, we shall invite others into His presence. We shall seek to present to them the attractions of Christ and the unseen realities of the world to come. There will be an intensity of desire to follow in the path that Jesus trod. There will be an earnest longing that those around us may "behold the Lamb of God, which taketh away the sin of the world." John 1:29.

And the effort to bless others will react in blessings upon ourselves. This was the purpose of God in giving us a part to act in the plan of redemption. He has granted men the privilege of becoming partakers of the divine nature and, in their turn, of diffusing blessings to their fellow men. This is the highest honor, the greatest joy, that it is possible for God to bestow upon men. Those who thus become participants in labors of love are brought nearest to their Creator.

God might have committed the message of the gospel, and all the work of loving ministry, to the heavenly angels. He might have employed other means for accomplishing His purpose. But in His infinite love He chose to make us co-workers with Himself, with Christ and the angels, that we might share the blessing, the joy, the spiritual uplifting, which results from this unselfish ministry.

We are brought into sympathy with Christ through the fellowship of His sufferings. Every act of self-sacrifice for the good of others strengthens the spirit of beneficence in the giver's heart, allying him more closely to the Redeemer of the world, who "was rich, yet for your sakes . . . became poor, that ye through His poverty might be rich." 2 Corinthians 8:9. And it is only as we thus fulfill the divine purpose in our creation that life can be a blessing to us.

If you will go to work as Christ designs that His disciples shall, and win souls for Him, you will feel the need of a deeper experience and a greater knowledge in divine things, and will hunger and thirst after righteousness. You will plead with God, and your faith will be strengthened, and your soul will drink deeper drafts at the well of salvation. Encountering opposition and trials will drive you to the Bible and prayer. You will grow in grace and the knowledge of Christ, and will develop a rich experience.

The spirit of unselfish labor for others gives depth, stability, and Christlike loveliness to the character, and brings peace and happiness to its possessor. The aspirations are elevated. There is no room for sloth or selfishness. Those who thus exercise the Christian graces will grow and will become strong to work for God. They will have clear spiritual perceptions, a steady, growing faith, and an increased power in prayer. The Spirit of God, moving upon their spirit, calls forth the sacred harmonies of the soul in answer to the divine touch. Those who thus devote themselves to unselfish effort for the good of others are most surely working out their own salvation.

The only way to grow in grace is to be disinterestedly doing the very work which Christ has enjoined upon us—to engage, to the extent of our ability, in helping and blessing those who need the help we can give them. Strength comes by exercise; activity is the very condition of life. Those who endeavor to maintain Christian life by passively accepting the blessings that come through the means of grace, and doing nothing for Christ, are simply trying to live by eating without working. And in the spiritual as in the natural world, this always results in degeneration and decay. A man who would refuse to exercise his limbs would soon lose all power to use them. Thus the Christian who will not exercise his God-given powers not only fails to grow up into Christ, but he loses the strength that he already had.

The church of Christ is God's appointed agency for the salvation of men. Its mission is to carry the gospel to the world. And the obligation rests upon all Christians. Everyone, to the extent of his talent and opportunity, is to fulfill the Saviour's commission. The love of Christ, revealed to us, makes us debtors to all who know Him not. God has given us light, not for ourselves alone, but to shed upon them.

If the followers of Christ were awake to duty, there would be thousands where there is one today proclaiming the gospel in heathen lands. And all who could not personally engage in the work, would yet sustain it with their means, their sympathy, and their prayers. And there would be far more earnest labor for souls in Christian countries.

We need not go to heathen lands, or even leave the narrow circle of the home, if it is there that our duty lies, in order to work for Christ. We can do this in the home circle, in the church, among those with whom we associate, and with whom we do business.

The greater part of our Saviour's life on earth was spent in patient toil in the carpenter's shop at Nazareth. Ministering angels attended the Lord of life as He walked side by side with peasants and laborers, unrecognized and un-honored. He was as faithfully fulfilling His mission while working at His humble trade as when He healed the sick or walked upon the storm-tossed waves of Galilee. So in the humblest duties and lowliest positions of life, we may walk and work with Jesus.

The apostle says, "Let every man, wherein he is called, therein abide with God." 1 Corinthians 7:24. The businessman may conduct his business in a way that will glorify his Master because of his fidelity. If he is a true follower of Christ he will carry his religion into everything that is done and reveal to men the spirit of Christ. The mechanic may be a diligent and faithful representative of Him who toiled in the lowly walks of life among the hills of Galilee. Everyone who names the name of Christ should so work that others, by seeing his good works, may be led to glorify their Creator and Redeemer.

Many have excused themselves from rendering their gifts to the service of Christ because others were possessed of superior endowments and advantages. The opinion has prevailed that only those who are especially talented are required to consecrate their abilities to the service of God. It has come to be understood by many that talents are given to only a certain favored class to the exclusion of others who of course are not called upon to share in the toils or the rewards. But it is not so represented in the parable. When the master of the house called his servants, he gave to every man *his* work.

With a loving spirit we may perform life's humblest duties "as to the Lord." Colossians 3:23. If the love of God is in the heart, it will be manifested in the life. The sweet savor of Christ will surround us, and our influence will elevate and bless.

You are not to wait for great occasions or to expect extraordinary abilities before you go to work for God. You need not have a thought of what the world will think of you. If your daily life is a testimony to the purity and sincerity of your faith, and others are convinced that you desire to benefit them, your efforts will not be wholly lost.

The humblest and poorest of the disciples of Jesus can be a blessing to others. They may not realize that they are doing any special good, but by their unconscious influence they may start waves of blessing that will widen and deepen, and the blessed results they may never know until the day of final reward. They do not feel or know that they are doing anything great. They are not required to weary themselves with anxiety about success. They have only to go forward quietly, doing faithfully the work that God's providence assigns, and their life will not be in vain. Their own souls will be growing more and more into the likeness of Christ; they are workers together with God in this life and are thus fitting for the higher work and the unshadowed joy of the life to come.

10

A Knowledge of God

Many are the ways in which God is seeking to make Himself known to us and bring us into communion with Him. Nature speaks to our senses without ceasing. The open heart will be impressed with the love and glory of God as revealed through the works of His hands. The listening ear can hear and understand the communications of God through the things of nature. The green fields, the lofty trees, the buds and flowers, the passing cloud, the falling rain, the babbling brook, the glories of the heavens, speak to our hearts, and invite us to become acquainted with Him who made them all.

Our Saviour bound up His precious lessons with the things of nature. The trees, the birds, the flowers of the valleys, the hills, the lakes, and the beautiful heavens, as well as the incidents and surroundings of daily life, were all linked with the words of truth, that His lessons might thus be often recalled to mind, even amid the busy cares of man's life of toil.

God would have His children appreciate His works and delight in the simple, quiet beauty with which He has adorned our earthly home. He is a lover of the beautiful, and above all that is outwardly attractive He loves beauty of character; He would have us cultivate purity and simplicity, the quiet graces of the flowers.

If we will but listen, God's created works will teach us precious lessons of obedience and trust. From the stars that in their trackless courses through space follow from age to age their appointed path, down to the minutest atom, the things of nature obey the Creator's will. And God cares for everything and sustains everything that He has created. He who upholds the unnumbered worlds throughout immensity, at the same time cares for the wants of the little brown sparrow that sings its humble song without fear. When men go forth to their daily toil, as when they engage in prayer; when they lie down at night, and when they rise in the morning; when the rich man feasts in his palace, or when the poor man gathers his children about the scanty board, each is tenderly watched by the heavenly Father. No tears are shed that God does not notice. There is no smile that He does not mark.

If we would but fully believe this, all undue anxieties would be dismissed. Our lives would not be so filled with disappointment as now; for everything, whether great or small, would be left in the hands of God, who is not perplexed by the multiplicity of cares, or overwhelmed by their weight. We should then enjoy a rest of soul to which many have long been strangers.

As your senses delight in the attractive loveliness of the earth, think of the world that is to come, that shall never know the blight of sin and death; where the face of nature will no more wear the shadow of the curse. Let your imagination picture the home of the saved, and remember that it will be more glorious than your brightest imagination can portray. In the varied gifts of God in nature we see but the faintest gleaming of His glory. It is written, "Eye hath not seen, nor ear heard, neither have entered into the heart of man, the things which God hath prepared for them that love Him." 1 Corinthians 2:9.

The poet and the naturalist have many things to say about nature, but it is the Christian who enjoys the beauty of the earth with the highest appreciation, because he recognizes his Father's handiwork and perceives His love in flower and shrub and tree. No one can fully appreciate the significance of hill and vale, river and sea, who does not look upon them as an expression of God's love to man.

God speaks to us through His providential workings and through the influence of His Spirit upon the heart. In our circumstances and surroundings, in the changes daily taking place around us, we may find precious lessons if our hearts are but open to discern them. The psalmist, tracing the work of God's providence, says, "The earth is full of the goodness of the Lord." "Whoso is wise, and will observe these things, even they shall understand the loving-kindness of the Lord." Psalm 33:5; 107:43.

God speaks to us in His word. Here we have in clearer lines the revelation of His character, of His dealings with men, and the great work of redemption. Here is open before us the history of patriarchs and prophets and other holy men of old. They were men "subject to like passions as we are." James 5:17. We see how they struggled through discouragements like our own, how they fell under temptation as we have done, and yet took heart again and conquered through the grace of God; and, beholding, we are encouraged in our striving after righteousness. As we read of the precious experiences granted them, of the light and love and blessing it was theirs to enjoy, and of the work they wrought through the grace given them, the spirit that inspired them kindles a flame of holy emulation in our hearts and a desire to be like them in charac-ter—like them to walk with God.

Jesus said of the Old Testament Scriptures,—and how much more is it true of the New,—"They are they which testify of Me," the Redeemer, Him in whom our hopes of eternal life are centered. John 5:39. Yes, the whole Bible tells of Christ. From the first record of creation—for "without Him was not anything made that was made"—to the closing promise, "Behold, I come quickly," we are reading of His works and listening to His voice. John 1:3; Revelation 22:12. If you would become acquainted with the Saviour, study the Holy Scriptures.

Fill the whole heart with the words of God. They are the living water, quenching your burning thirst. They are the living bread from heaven. Jesus declares, "Except ye eat the flesh of the Son of man, and drink His blood, ye have no life in you." And He explains Himself by saying, "The words that I speak unto you, they are spirit, and they are life." John 6:53, 63. Our bodies are built up from what we eat and drink; and as in the natural economy, so in the spiritual economy: it is what we meditate upon that will give tone and strength to our spiritual nature.

The theme of redemption is one that the angels desire to look into; it will be the science and the song of the redeemed throughout the ceaseless ages of eternity. Is it not worthy of careful thought and study now? The infinite mercy and love of Jesus, the sacrifice made in our behalf, call for the most serious and solemn reflection. We should dwell upon the character of our dear Redeemer and Intercessor. We should meditate upon the mission of Him who came to save His people from their sins. As we thus contemplate heavenly themes, our faith and love will grow stronger, and our prayers will be more and more acceptable to God, because they will be more and more mixed with faith and love. They will be intelligent and fervent. There will be more constant confidence in Jesus, and a daily, living experience in His power to save to the uttermost all that come unto God by Him.

As we meditate upon the perfections of the Saviour, we shall desire to be wholly transformed and renewed in the image of His purity. There will be a hungering and thirsting of soul to become like Him whom we adore. The more our thoughts are upon Christ, the more we shall speak of Him to others and represent Him to the world.

The Bible was not written for the scholar alone; on the contrary, it was designed for the common people. The great truths necessary for salvation are made as clear as noonday; and none will mistake and lose their way except those who follow their own judgment instead of the plainly revealed will of God.

We should not take the testimony of any man as to what the Scriptures teach, but should study the words of God for ourselves. If we allow others to do our thinking, we shall have crippled energies and contracted abilities. The noble powers of the mind may be so dwarfed by lack of exercise on themes worthy of their concentration as to lose their ability to grasp the deep meaning of the word of God. The mind will enlarge if it is employed in tracing out the relation of the subjects of the Bible, comparing scripture with scripture and spiritual things with spiritual.

There is nothing more calculated to strengthen the intellect than the study of the Scriptures. No other book is so potent to elevate the thoughts, to give vigor to the faculties, as the broad, ennobling truths of the Bible. If God's word were studied as it should be, men would have a breadth of mind, a nobility of character, and a stability of purpose rarely seen in these times.

But there is but little benefit derived from a hasty reading of the Scriptures. One may read the whole Bible through and yet fail to see its beauty or comprehend its deep and hidden meaning. One passage studied until its significance is clear to the mind and its relation to the plan of salvation is evident, is of more value than the perusal of many chapters with no definite purpose in view and no positive instruction gained. Keep your Bible with you. As you have opportunity, read it; fix the texts in your memory. Even while you are walking the streets you may read a passage and meditate upon it, thus fixing it in the mind.

We cannot obtain wisdom without earnest attention and prayerful study. Some portions of Scripture are indeed too plain to be misunderstood, but there are others whose meaning does not lie on the surface to be seen at a glance. Scripture must be compared with scripture. There must be careful research and prayerful reflection. And such study will be richly repaid. As the miner discovers veins of precious metal concealed beneath the surface of the earth, so will he who perseveringly searches the word of God as for hid treasure find truths of the greatest value, which are concealed from the view of the careless seeker. The words of inspiration, pondered in the heart, will be as streams flowing from the fountain of life.

Never should the Bible be studied without prayer. Before opening its pages we should ask for the enlightenment of the Holy Spirit, and it will be given. When Nathanael came to Jesus, the Saviour exclaimed, "Behold an Israelite indeed, in whom is no guile!" Nathanael said, "Whence knowest Thou me?" Jesus answered, "Before that Philip called thee, when thou wast under the fig tree, I saw thee." John 1:47, 48. And Jesus will see us also in the secret places of prayer if we will seek Him for light that we may know what is truth. Angels from the world of light will be with those who in humility of heart seek for divine guidance.

The Holy Spirit exalts and glorifies the Saviour. It is His office to present Christ, the purity of His righteousness, and the great salvation that we have through Him. Jesus says, "He shall receive of Mine, and shall show it unto you." John 16:14. The Spirit of truth is the only effectual teacher of divine truth. How must God esteem the human race, since He gave His Son to die for them and appoints His Spirit to be man's teacher and continual guide!

11

The Privilege of Prayer

Through nature and revelation, through His providence, and by the influence of His Spirit, God speaks to us. But these are not enough; we need also to pour out our hearts to Him. In order to have spiritual life and energy, we must have actual intercourse with our heavenly Father. Our minds may be drawn out toward Him; we may meditate upon His works, His mercies, His blessings; but this is not, in the fullest sense, communing with Him. In order to commune with God, we must have something to say to Him concerning our actual life.

Prayer is the opening of the heart to God as to a friend. Not that it is necessary in order to make known to God what we are, but in order to enable us to receive Him. Prayer does not bring God down to us, but brings us up to Him.

When Jesus was upon the earth, He taught His disciples how to pray. He directed them to present their daily needs before God, and to cast all their care upon Him. And the assurance He gave them that their petitions should be heard, is assurance also to us.

Jesus Himself, while He dwelt among men, was often in prayer. Our Saviour identified Himself with our needs and weakness, in that He became a suppliant, a petitioner, seeking from His Father fresh supplies of strength, that He might come forth braced for duty and trial. He is our example in all things. He is a brother in our infirmities, "in all points tempted like as we are;" but as the sinless one His nature recoiled from evil; He endured struggles and torture of soul in a world of sin. His humanity made prayer a necessity and a privilege. He found comfort and joy in communion with His Father. And if the Saviour of men, the Son of God, felt the need of prayer, how much more should feeble, sinful mortals feel the necessity of fervent, constant prayer.

Our heavenly Father waits to bestow upon us the fullness of His blessing. It is our privilege to drink largely at the fountain of boundless love. What a wonder it is that we pray so little! God is ready and willing to hear the sincere prayer of the humblest of His children, and yet there is much manifest reluctance on our part to make known our wants to God. What can the angels of heaven think of poor helpless human beings, who are subject to temptation, when God's heart of infinite love yearns toward them, ready to give them more than they can ask or think, and yet they pray so little and have so little faith? The angels love to bow before God; they love to be near Him. They regard communion with God as their highest joy; and yet the children of earth, who need so much the help that God only can give, seem satisfied to walk without the light of His Spirit, the companionship of His presence.

The darkness of the evil one encloses those who neglect to pray. The whispered temptations of the enemy entice them to sin; and it is all because they do not make use of the privileges that God has given them in the divine appointment of prayer. Why should the sons and daughters of God be reluctant to pray, when prayer is the key in the hand of faith to unlock heaven's storehouse, where are treasured the boundless resources of Omnipotence? Without unceasing prayer and diligent watching we are in danger of growing careless and of deviating from the right path. The adversary seeks continually to obstruct the way to the mercy seat, that we may not by earnest supplication and faith obtain grace and power to resist temptation.

There are certain conditions upon which we may expect that God will hear and answer our prayers. One of the first of these is that we feel our need of help from Him. He has promised, "I will pour water upon him that is thirsty, and floods upon the dry ground." Isaiah 44:3. Those who hunger and thirst after righteousness, who long after God, may be sure that they will be filled. The heart must be open to the Spirit's influence, or God's blessing cannot be received.

Our great need is itself an argument and pleads most eloquently in our behalf. But the Lord is to be sought unto to do these things for us. He says, "Ask, and it shall be given you." And "He that spared not His own Son, but delivered Him up for us all, how shall He not with Him also freely give us all things?" Matthew 7:7; Romans 8:32.

If we regard iniquity in our hearts, if we cling to any known sin, the Lord will not hear us; but the prayer of the penitent, contrite soul is always accepted. When all known wrongs are righted, we may believe that God will answer our petitions. Our own merit will never commend us to the favor of God; it is the worthiness of Jesus that will save us, His blood that will cleanse us; yet we have a work to do in complying with the conditions of acceptance.

Another element of prevailing prayer is faith. "He that cometh to God must believe that He is, and that He is a rewarder of them that diligently seek Him." Hebrews 11:6. Jesus said to His disciples, "What things soever ye desire, when ye pray, believe that ye receive them, and ye shall have them." Mark 11:24. Do we take Him at His word?

The assurance is broad and unlimited, and He is faithful who has promised. When we do not receive the very things we asked for, at the time we ask, we are still to believe that the Lord hears and that He will answer our prayers. We are so erring and short-sighted that we sometimes ask for things that would not be a blessing to us, and our heavenly Father in love answers our prayers by giving us that which will be for our highest good—that which we ourselves would desire if with vision divinely enlightened we could see all things as they really are. When our prayers seem not to be answered, we are to cling to the promise; for the time of answering will surely come, and we shall receive the blessing we need most. But to claim that prayer will always be answered in the very way and for the particular thing that we desire, is presumption. God is too wise to err, and too good to withhold any good thing from them that walk uprightly. Then do not fear to trust Him, even though you do not see the immediate answer to your prayers. Rely upon His sure promise, "Ask, and it shall be given you."

If we take counsel with our doubts and fears, or try to solve everything that we cannot see clearly, before we have faith, perplexities will only increase and deepen. But if we come to God, feeling helpless and dependent, as we really are, and in humble, trusting faith make known our wants to Him whose knowledge is infinite, who sees everything in creation, and who governs everything by His will and word, He can and will attend to our cry, and will let light shine into our hearts. Through sincere prayer we are brought into connection with the mind of the Infinite. We may have no remarkable evidence at the time that the face of our Redeemer is bending over us in compassion and love, but this is even so. We may not feel His visible touch, but His hand is upon us in love and pitying tenderness.

When we come to ask mercy and blessing from God we should have a spirit of love and forgiveness in our own hearts. How can we pray, "Forgive us our debts, *as* we forgive our debtors," and yet indulge an unforgiving spirit? Matthew 6:12. If we expect our own prayers to be heard we must forgive others in the same manner and to the same extent as we hope to be forgiven.

Perseverance in prayer has been made a condition of receiving. We must pray always if we would grow in faith and experience. We are to be "instant in prayer," to "continue in prayer, and watch in the same with thanksgiving." Romans 12:12; Colossians 4:2. Peter exhorts believers to be "sober, and watch unto prayer." 1 Peter 4:7. Paul directs, "In everything by prayer and supplication with thanksgiving let your requests be made known unto God." Philippians 4:6. "But ye, beloved," says Jude, "praying in the Holy Ghost, keep yourselves in the love of God." Jude 20, 21. Unceasing prayer is the unbroken union of the soul with God, so that life from God flows into our life; and from our life, purity and holiness flow back to God.

There is necessity for diligence in prayer; let nothing hinder you. Make every effort to keep open the communion between Jesus and your own soul. Seek every opportunity to go where prayer is wont to be made. Those who are really seeking for communion with God will be seen in the prayer meeting, faithful to do their duty and earnest and anxious to reap all the benefits they can gain. They will improve every opportunity of placing themselves where they can receive the rays of light from heaven.

We should pray in the family circle, and above all we must not neglect secret prayer, for this is the life of the soul. It is impossible for the soul to flourish while prayer is neglected. Family or public prayer alone is not sufficient. In solitude let the soul be laid open to the inspecting eye of God. Secret prayer is to be heard only by the prayer-hearing God. No curious ear is to receive the burden of such petitions. In secret prayer the soul is free from surrounding influences, free from excitement. Calmly, yet fervently, will it reach out after God. Sweet and abiding will be the influence emanating from Him who seeth in secret, whose ear is open to hear the prayer arising from the heart. By calm, simple faith the soul holds communion with God and gathers to itself rays of divine light to strengthen and sustain it in the conflict with Satan. God is our tower of strength.

Pray in your closet, and as you go about your daily labor let your heart be often uplifted to God. It was thus that Enoch walked with God. These silent prayers rise like precious incense before the throne of grace. Satan cannot overcome him whose heart is thus stayed upon God.

There is no time or place in which it is inappropriate to offer up a petition to God. There is nothing that can prevent us from lifting up our hearts in the spirit of earnest prayer. In the crowds of the street, in the midst of a business engagement, we may send up a petition to God and plead for divine guidance, as did Nehemiah when he made his request before King Artaxerxes. A closet of communion may be found wherever we are. We should have the door of the heart open continually and our invitation going up that Jesus may come and abide as a heavenly guest in the soul.

Although there may be a tainted, corrupted atmosphere around us, we need not breathe its miasma, but may live in the pure air of heaven. We may close every door to impure imaginings and unholy thoughts by lifting the soul into the presence of God through sincere prayer. Those whose hearts are open to receive the support and blessing of God will walk in a holier atmosphere than that of earth and will have constant communion with heaven.

We need to have more distinct views of Jesus and a fuller comprehension of the value of eternal realities. The beauty of holiness is to fill the hearts of God's children; and that this may be accomplished, we should seek for divine disclosures of heavenly things.

Let the soul be drawn out and upward, that God may grant us a breath of the heavenly atmosphere. We may keep so near to God that in every unexpected trial our thoughts will turn to Him as naturally as the flower turns to the sun.

Keep your wants, your joys, your sorrows, your cares, and your fears before God. You cannot burden Him; you cannot weary Him. He who numbers the hairs of your head is not indifferent to the wants of His children. "The Lord is very pitiful, and of tender mercy." James 5:11. His heart of love is touched by our sorrows and even by our utterances of them. Take to Him everything that perplexes the mind. Nothing is too great for Him to bear, for He holds up worlds, He rules over all the affairs of the universe. Nothing that in any way concerns our peace is too small for Him to notice. There is no chapter in our experience too dark for Him to read; there is no perplexity too difficult for Him to unravel. No calamity can befall the least of His children, no anxiety harass the soul, no joy cheer, no sincere prayer escape the lips, of which our heavenly Father is unobservant, or in which He takes no immediate interest. "He healeth the broken in heart, and bindeth up their wounds." Psalm 147:3. The relations between God and each soul are as distinct and full as though there were not another soul upon the earth to share His watchcare, not another soul for whom He gave His beloved Son.

Jesus said, "Ye shall ask in My name: and I say not unto you, that I will pray the Father for you: for the Father Himself loveth you." "I have chosen you: . . . that whatsoever ye shall ask of the Father in My name, He may give it you." John 16:26, 27; 15:16. But to pray in the name of Jesus is something more than a mere mention of that name at the beginning and the ending of a prayer. It is to pray in the mind and spirit of Jesus, while we believe His promises, rely upon His grace, and work His works.

God does not mean that any of us should become hermits or monks and retire from the world in order to devote ourselves to acts of worship. The life must be like Christ's life—between the mountain and the multitude. He who does nothing but pray will soon cease to pray, or his prayers will become a formal routine. When men take themselves out of social life, away from the sphere of Christian duty and cross bearing; when they cease to work earnestly for the Master, who worked earnestly for them, they lose the subject matter of prayer and have no incentive to devotion. Their prayers become personal and selfish. They cannot pray in regard to the wants of humanity or the upbuilding of Christ's kingdom, pleading for strength wherewith to work.

We sustain a loss when we neglect the privilege of associating together to strengthen and encourage one another in the service of God. The truths of His word lose their vividness and importance in our minds. Our hearts cease to be enlightened and aroused by their sanctifying influence, and we decline in spirituality. In our association as Christians we lose much by lack of sympathy with one another. He who shuts himself up to himself is not filling the position that God designed he should. The proper cultivation of the social elements in our nature brings us into sympathy with others and is a means of development and strength to us in the service of God.

If Christians would associate together, speaking to each other of the love of God and of the precious truths of redemption, their own hearts would be refreshed and they would refresh one another. We may be daily learning more of our heavenly Father, gaining a fresh experience of His grace; then we shall desire to speak of His love; and as we do this, our own hearts will be warmed and encouraged. If we thought and talked more of Jesus, and less of self, we should have far more of His presence.

If we would but think of God as often as we have evidence of His care for us we should keep Him ever in our thoughts and should delight to talk of Him and to praise Him. We talk of temporal things because we have an interest in them. We talk of our friends because we love them; our joys and our sorrows are bound up with them. Yet we have infinitely greater reason to love God than to love our earthly friends; it should be the most natural thing in the world to make Him first in all our thoughts, to talk of His goodness and tell of His power. The rich gifts He has bestowed upon us were not intended to absorb our thoughts and love so much that we should have nothing to give to God; they are constantly to remind us of Him and to bind us in bonds of love and gratitude to our heavenly Benefactor. We dwell too near the lowlands of earth.

Let us raise our eyes to the open door of the sanctuary above, where the light of the glory of God shines in the face of Christ, who "is able also to save them to the uttermost that come unto God by Him." Hebrews 7:25.

We need to praise God more "for His goodness, and for His wonderful works to the children of men." Psalm 107:8. Our devotional exercises should not consist wholly in asking and receiving. Let us not be always thinking of our wants and never of the benefits we receive. We do not pray any too much, but we are too sparing of giving thanks. We are the constant recipients of God's mercies, and yet how little gratitude we express, how little we praise Him for what He has done for us.

Anciently the Lord bade Israel, when they met together for His service, "Ye shall eat before the Lord your God, and ye shall rejoice in all that ye put your hand unto, ye and your households, wherein the Lord thy God hath blessed thee." Deuteronomy 12:7. That which is done for the glory of God should be done with cheerfulness, with songs of praise and thanksgiving, not with sadness and gloom.

Our God is a tender, merciful Father. His service should not be looked upon as a heart-saddening, distressing exercise. It should be a pleasure to worship the Lord and to take part in His work. God would not have His children, for whom so great salvation has been provided, act as if He were a hard, exacting taskmaster. He is their best friend; and when they worship Him, He expects to be with them, to bless and comfort them, filling their hearts with joy and love. The Lord desires His children to take comfort in His service and to find more pleasure than hardship in His work. He desires that those who come to worship Him shall carry away with them precious thoughts of His care and love, that they may be cheered in all the employments of daily life, that they may have grace to deal honestly and faithfully in all things.

We must gather about the cross. Christ and Him crucified should be the theme of contemplation, of conversation, and of our most joyful emotion. We should keep in our thoughts every blessing we receive from God, and when we realize His great love we should be willing to trust everything to the hand that was nailed to the cross for us.

The soul may ascend nearer heaven on the wings of praise. God is worshiped with song and music in the courts above, and as we express our gratitude we are approximating to the worship of the heavenly hosts. "Whoso offereth praise glorifieth" God. Psalm 50:23. Let us with reverent joy come before our Creator, with "thanksgiving, and the voice of melody." Isaiah 51:3.

12

What to do with Doubt

Many, especially those who are young in the Christian life, are at times troubled with the suggestions of skepticism. There are in the Bible many things which they cannot explain, or even understand, and Satan employs these to shake their faith in the Scriptures as a revelation from God. They ask, "How shall I know the right way? If the Bible is indeed the word of God, how can I be freed from these doubts and perplexities?"

God never asks us to believe, without giving sufficient evidence upon which to base our faith. His existence, His character, the truthfulness of His word, are all established by testimony that appeals to our reason; and this testimony is abundant. Yet God has never removed the possibility of doubt. Our faith must rest upon evidence, not demonstration. Those who wish to doubt will have opportunity; while those who really desire to know the truth will find plenty of evidence on which to rest their faith.

It is impossible for finite minds fully to comprehend the character or the works of the Infinite One. To the keenest intellect, the most highly educated mind, that holy Being must ever remain clothed in mystery. "Canst thou by searching find out God? canst thou find out the Almighty unto perfection? It is as high as heaven; what canst thou do? deeper than hell; what canst thou know?" Job 11:7, 8.

The apostle Paul exclaims, "O the depth of the riches both of the wisdom and knowledge of God! how unsearchable are His judgments, and His ways past finding out!" Romans 11:33. But though "clouds and darkness are round about Him," "righteousness and judgment are the foundation of His throne." Psalm 97:2, R.V. We can so far comprehend His dealings with us, and the motives by which He is actuated, that we may discern boundless love and mercy united to infinite power. We can understand as much of His purposes as it is for our good to know; and beyond this we must still trust the hand that is omnipotent, the heart that is full of love.

The word of God, like the character of its divine Author, presents mysteries that can never be fully comprehended by finite beings. The entrance of sin into the world, the incarnation of Christ, regeneration, the resurrection, and many other subjects presented in the Bible, are mysteries too deep for the human mind to explain, or even fully to comprehend. But we have no reason to doubt God's word because we cannot understand the mysteries of His providence. In the natural world we are constantly surrounded with mysteries that we cannot fathom. The very humblest forms of life present a problem that the wisest of philosophers is powerless to explain. Everywhere are wonders beyond our ken. Should we then be surprised to find that in the spiritual world also there are mysteries that we cannot fathom? The difficulty lies solely in the weakness and narrowness of the human mind. God has given us in the Scriptures sufficient evidence of their divine character, and we are not to doubt His word because we cannot understand all the mysteries of His providence.

The apostle Peter says that there are in Scripture "things hard to be understood, which they that are unlearned and unstable wrest . . . unto their own destruction." 2 Peter 3:16. The difficulties of Scripture have been urged by skeptics as an argument against the Bible; but so far from this, they constitute a strong evidence of its divine inspiration. If it contained no account of God but that which we could easily comprehend; if His greatness and majesty could be grasped by finite minds, then the Bible would not bear the unmistakable credentials of divine authority. The very grandeur and mystery of the themes presented should inspire faith in it as the word of God.

The Bible unfolds truth with a simplicity and a perfect adaptation to the needs and longings of the human heart, that has astonished and charmed the most highly cultivated minds, while it enables the humblest and uncultured to discern the way of salvation. And yet these simply stated truths lay hold upon subjects so elevated, so far-reaching, so infinitely beyond the power of human comprehension, that we can accept them only because God has declared them. Thus the plan of redemption is laid open to us, so that every soul may see the steps he is to take in repentance toward God and faith toward our Lord Jesus Christ, in order to be saved in God's appointed way; yet beneath these truths, so easily understood, lie mysteries that are the hiding of His glory—mysteries that overpower the mind in its research, yet inspire the sincere seeker for truth with reverence and faith. The more he searches the Bible, the deeper is his conviction that it is the word of the living God, and human reason bows before the majesty of divine revelation.

To acknowledge that we cannot fully comprehend the great truths of the Bible is only to admit that the finite mind is inadequate to grasp the infinite; that man, with his limited, human knowledge, cannot understand the purposes of Omniscience.

Because they cannot fathom all its mysteries, the skeptic and the infidel reject God's word; and not all who profess to believe the Bible are free from danger on this point. The apostle says, "Take heed, brethren, lest there be in any of you an evil heart of unbelief, in departing from the living God." Hebrews 3:12. It is right to study closely the teachings of the Bible and to search into "the deep things of God" so far as they are revealed in Scripture. 1 Corinthians 2:10. While "the secret things belong unto the Lord our God," "those things which are revealed belong unto us." Deuteronomy 29:29. But it is Satan's work to pervert the investigative powers of the mind. A certain pride is mingled with the consideration of Bible truth, so that men feel impatient and defeated if they cannot explain every portion of Scripture to their satisfaction. It is too humiliating to them to acknowledge that they do not understand the inspired words. They are unwilling to wait patiently until God shall see fit to reveal the truth to them. They feel that their unaided human wisdom is sufficient to enable them to comprehend the Scripture, and failing to do this, they virtually deny its authority. It is true that many theories and doctrines popularly supposed to be derived from the Bible have no foundation in its teaching, and indeed are contrary to the whole tenor of inspiration. These things have been a cause of doubt and perplexity to many minds. They are not, however, chargeable to God's word, but to man's perversion of it.

If it were possible for created beings to attain to a full understanding of God and His works, then, having reached this point, there would be for them no further discovery of truth, no growth in knowledge, no further development of mind or heart. God would no longer be supreme; and man, having reached the limit of knowledge and attainment, would cease to advance. Let us thank God that it is not so. God is infinite; in Him are "all the treasures of wisdom and knowledge." Colossians 2:3. And to all eternity men may be ever searching, ever learning, and yet never exhaust the treasures of His wisdom, His goodness, and His power.

God intends that even in this life the truths of His word shall be ever unfolding to His people. There is only one way in which this knowledge can be obtained. We can attain to an understanding of God's word only through the illumination of that Spirit by which the word was given. "The things of God knoweth no man, but the Spirit of God;" "for the Spirit searcheth all things, yea, the deep things of God." 1 Corinthians 2:11, 10. And the Saviour's promise to His followers was, "When He, the Spirit of truth, is come, He will guide you into all truth. . . . For He shall receive of Mine, and shall show it unto you." John 16:13, 14.

God desires man to exercise his reasoning powers; and the study of the Bible will strengthen and elevate the mind as no other study can. Yet we are to beware of deifying reason, which is subject to the weakness and infirmity of humanity. If we would not have the Scriptures clouded to our understanding, so that the plainest truths shall not be comprehended, we must have the simplicity and faith of a little child, ready to learn, and beseeching the aid of the Holy Spirit. A sense of the power and wisdom of God, and of our inability to comprehend His greatness, should inspire us with humility, and we should open His word, as we would enter His presence, with holy awe. When we come to the Bible, reason must acknowledge an authority superior to itself, and heart and intellect must bow to the great I AM.

There are many things apparently difficult or obscure, which God will make plain and simple to those who thus seek an understanding of them. But without the guidance of the Holy Spirit we shall be continually liable to wrest the Scriptures or to misinterpret them. There is much reading of the Bible that is without profit and in many cases a positive injury. When the word of God is opened without reverence and without prayer; when the thoughts and affections are not fixed upon God, or in harmony with His will, the mind is clouded with doubts; and in the very study of the Bible, skepticism strengthens. The enemy takes control of the thoughts, and he suggests interpretations that are not correct. Whenever men are not in word and deed seeking to be in harmony with God, then, however learned they may be, they are liable to err in their understanding of Scripture, and it is not safe to trust to their explanations. Those who look to the Scriptures to find discrepancies, have not spiritual insight. With distorted vision they will see many causes for doubt and unbelief in things that are really plain and simple.

Disguise it as they may, the real cause of doubt and skepticism, in most cases, is the love of sin. The teachings and restrictions of God's word are not welcome to the proud, sin-loving heart, and those who are unwilling to obey its requirements are ready to doubt its authority. In order to arrive at truth, we must have a sincere desire to know the truth and a willingness of heart to obey it. And all who come in this spirit to the study of the Bible will find abundant evidence that it is God's word, and they may gain an understanding of its truths that will make them wise unto salvation.

Christ has said, "If any man willeth to do His will, he shall know of the teaching." John 7:17, R.V. Instead of questioning and caviling concerning that which you do not understand, give heed to the light that already shines upon you, and you will receive greater light. By the grace of Christ, perform every duty that has been made plain to your understanding, and you will be enabled to understand and perform those of which you are now in doubt.

There is an evidence that is open to all,—the most highly educated, and the most illiterate,—the evidence of experience. God invites us to prove for ourselves the reality of His word, the truth of His promises. He bids us "taste and see that the Lord is good." Psalm 34:8. Instead of depending upon the word of another, we are to taste for ourselves. He declares, "Ask, and ye shall receive." John 16:24. His promises will be fulfilled. They have never failed; they never can fail. And as we draw near to Jesus, and rejoice in the fullness of His love, our doubt and darkness will disappear in the light of His presence.

The apostle Paul says that God "hath delivered us from the power of darkness, and hath translated us into the kingdom of His dear Son." Colossians 1:13. And everyone who has passed from death unto life is able to "set to his seal that God is true." John 3:33. He can testify, "I needed help, and I found it in Jesus. Every want was supplied, the hunger of my soul was satisfied; and now the Bible is to me the revelation of Jesus Christ. Do you ask why I believe in Jesus? Because He is to me a divine Saviour. Why do I believe the Bible? Because I have found it to be the voice of God to my soul." We may have the witness in ourselves that the Bible is true, that Christ is the Son of God. We know that we are not following cunningly devised fables.

Peter exhorts his brethren to "grow in grace, and in the knowledge of our Lord and Saviour Jesus Christ." 2 Peter 3:18. When the people of God are growing in grace, they will be constantly obtaining a clearer understanding of His word. They will discern new light and beauty in its sacred truths. This has been true in the history of the church in all ages, and thus it will continue to the end. "The path of the righteous is as the light of dawn, that shineth more and more unto the perfect day." Proverbs 4:18, R.V., margin.

By faith we may look to the hereafter and grasp the pledge of God for a growth of intellect, the human faculties uniting with the divine, and every power of the soul being brought into direct contact with the Source of light. We may rejoice that all which has perplexed us in the providences of God will then be made plain, things hard to be understood will then find an explanation; and where our finite minds discovered only confusion and broken purposes, we shall see the most perfect and beautiful harmony. "Now we see through a glass, darkly; but then face to face: now I know in part; but then shall I know even as also I am known." 1 Corinthians 13:12.

13
Rejoicing in the Lord

The children of God are called to be representatives of Christ, showing forth the goodness and mercy of the Lord. As Jesus has revealed to us the true character of the Father, so we are to reveal Christ to a world that does not know His tender, pitying love. "As Thou hast sent Me into the world," said Jesus, "even so have I also sent them into the world." "I in them, and Thou in Me; . . . that the world may know that Thou hast sent Me." John 17: 18, 23. The apostle Paul says to the disciples of Jesus, "Ye are manifestly declared to be the epistle of Christ," "known and read of all men." 2 Corinthians 3:3, 2. In every one of His children, Jesus sends a letter to the world. If you are Christ's follower, He sends in you a letter to the family, the village, the street, where you live. Jesus, dwelling in you, desires to speak to the hearts of those who are not acquainted with Him. Perhaps they do not read the Bible, or do not hear the voice that speaks to them in its pages; they do not see the love of God through His works. But if you are a true representative of Jesus, it may be that through you they will be led to understand something of His goodness and be won to love and serve Him.

Christians are set as light bearers on the way to heaven. They are to reflect to the world the light shining upon them from Christ. Their life and character should be such that through them others will get a right conception of Christ and of His service.

If we do represent Christ, we shall make His service appear attractive, as it really is. Christians who gather up gloom and sadness to their souls, and murmur and complain, are giving to others a false representation of God and the Christian life. They give the impression that God is not pleased to have His children happy, and in this they bear false witness against our heavenly Father.

Satan is exultant when he can lead the children of God into unbelief and despondency. He delights to see us mistrusting God, doubting His willingness and power to save us. He loves to have us feel that the Lord will do us harm by His providences. It is the work of Satan to represent the Lord as lacking in compassion and pity. He misstates the truth in regard to Him. He fills the imagination with false ideas concerning God; and instead of dwelling upon the truth in regard to our heavenly Father, we too often fix our minds upon the misrepresentations of Satan and dishonor God by distrusting Him and murmuring against Him. Satan ever seeks to make the religious life one of gloom. He desires it to appear toilsome and difficult; and when the Christian presents in his own life this view of religion, he is, through his unbelief, seconding the falsehood of Satan.

Many, walking along the path of life, dwell upon their mistakes and failures and disappointments, and their hearts are filled with grief and discouragement. While I was in Europe, a sister who had been doing this, and who was in deep distress, wrote to me, asking for some word of encouragement. The night after I had read her letter I dreamed that I was in a garden, and one who seemed to be the owner of the garden was conducting me through its paths. I was gathering the flowers and enjoying their fragrance, when this sister, who had been walking by my side, called my attention to some unsightly briers that were impeding her way. There she was mourning and grieving. She was not walking in the pathway, following the guide, but was walking among the briers and thorns. "Oh," she mourned, "is it not a pity that this beautiful garden is spoiled with thorns?" Then the guide said, "Let the thorns alone, for they will only wound you. Gather the roses, the lilies, and the pinks."

Have there not been some bright spots in your experience? Have you not had some precious seasons when your heart throbbed with joy in response to the Spirit of God? When you look back into the chapters of your life experience do you not find some pleasant pages? Are not God's promises, like the fragrant flowers, growing beside your path on every hand? Will you not let their beauty and sweetness fill your heart with joy?

The briers and thorns will only wound and grieve you; and if you gather only these things, and present them to others, are you not, besides slighting the goodness of God yourself, preventing those around you from walking in the path of life?

It is not wise to gather together all the unpleasant recollections of a past life,—its iniquities and disappointments,—to talk over them and mourn over them until we are overwhelmed with discouragement. A discouraged soul is filled with darkness, shutting out the light of God from his own soul and casting a shadow upon the pathway of others.

Thank God for the bright pictures which He has presented to us. Let us group together the blessed assurances of His love, that we may look upon them continually: The Son of God leaving His Father's throne, clothing His divinity with humanity, that He might rescue man from the power of Satan; His triumph in our behalf, opening heaven to men, revealing to human vision the presence chamber where the Deity unveils His glory; the fallen race uplifted from the pit of ruin into which sin had plunged it, and brought again into connection with the infinite God, and having endured the divine test through faith in our Redeemer, clothed in the righteousness of Christ, and exalted to His throne—these are the pictures which God would have us contemplate.

When we seem to doubt God's love and distrust His promises we dishonor Him and grieve His Holy Spirit. How would a mother feel if her children were constantly complaining of her, just as though she did not mean them well, when her whole life's effort had been to forward their interests and to give them comfort? Suppose they should doubt her love; it would break her heart. How would any parent feel to be thus treated by his children? And how can our heavenly Father regard us when we distrust His love, which has led Him to give His only-begotten Son that we might have life? The apostle writes, "He that spared not His own Son, but delivered Him up for us all, how shall He not with Him also freely give us all things?" Romans 8:32. And yet how many, by their actions, if not in word, are saying, "The Lord does not mean this for me. Perhaps He loves others, but He does not love me."

All this is harming your own soul; for every word of doubt you utter is inviting Satan's temptations; it is strengthening in you the tendency to doubt, and it is grieving from you the ministering angels. When Satan tempts you, breathe not a word of doubt or darkness. If you choose to open the door to his suggestions, your mind will be filled with distrust and rebellious questioning. If you talk out your feelings, every doubt you express not only reacts upon yourself, but it is a seed that will germinate and bear fruit in the life of others, and it may be impossible to counteract the influence of your words. You yourself may be able to recover from the season of temptation and from the snare of Satan, but others who have been swayed by your influence may not be able to escape from the unbelief you have suggested. How important that we speak only those things that will give spiritual strength and life!

Angels are listening to hear what kind of report you are bearing to the world about your heavenly Master. Let your conversation be of Him who liveth to make intercession for you before the Father. When you take the hand of a friend, let praise to God be on your lips and in your heart. This will attract his thoughts to Jesus.

All have trials; griefs hard to bear, temptations hard to resist. Do not tell your troubles to your fellow mortals, but carry everything to God in prayer. Make it a rule never to utter one word of doubt or discouragement. You can do much to brighten the life of others and strengthen their efforts, by words of hope and holy cheer.

There is many a brave soul sorely pressed by temptation, almost ready to faint in the conflict with self and with the powers of evil. Do not discourage such a one in his hard struggle. Cheer him with brave, hopeful words that shall urge him on his way. Thus the light of Christ may shine from you. "None of us liveth to himself." Romans 14:7. By our unconscious influence others may be encouraged and strengthened, or they may be discouraged, and repelled from Christ and the truth.

There are many who have an erroneous idea of the life and character of Christ. They think that He was devoid of warmth and sunniness, that He was stern, severe, and joyless. In many cases the whole religious experience is colored by these gloomy views.

It is often said that Jesus wept, but that He was never known to smile. Our Saviour was indeed a Man of Sorrows, and acquainted with grief, for He opened His heart to all the woes of men. But though His life was self-denying and shadowed with pain and care, His spirit was not crushed. His countenance did not wear an expression of grief and repining, but ever one of peaceful serenity. His heart was a wellspring of life, and wherever He went He carried rest and peace, joy and gladness.

Our Saviour was deeply serious and intensely in earnest, but never gloomy or morose. The life of those who imitate Him will be full of earnest purpose; they will have a deep sense of personal responsibility. Levity will be repressed; there will be no boisterous merriment, no rude jesting; but the religion of Jesus gives peace like a river. It does not quench the light of joy; it does not restrain cheerfulness nor cloud the sunny, smiling face. Christ came not to be ministered unto but to minister; and when His love reigns in the heart, we shall follow His example.

If we keep uppermost in our minds the unkind and unjust acts of others we shall find it impossible to love them as Christ has loved us; but if our thoughts dwell upon the wondrous love and pity of Christ for us, the same spirit will flow out to others. We should love and respect one another, notwithstanding the faults and imperfections that we cannot help seeing. Humility and self-distrust should be cultivated, and a patient tenderness with the faults of others. This will kill out all narrowing selfishness and make us large-hearted and generous.

The psalmist says, "Trust in the Lord, and do good; so shalt thou dwell in the land, and verily thou shalt be fed." Psalm 37:3. "Trust in the Lord." Each day has its burdens, its cares and perplexities; and when we meet how ready we are to talk of our difficulties and trials. So many borrowed troubles intrude, so many fears are indulged, such a weight of anxiety is expressed, that one might suppose we had no pitying, loving Saviour ready to hear all our requests and to be to us a present help in every time of need.

Some are always fearing, and borrowing trouble. Every day they are surrounded with the tokens of God's love; every day they are enjoying the bounties of His providence; but they overlook these present blessings. Their minds are continually dwelling upon something disagreeable which they fear may come; or some difficulty may really exist which, though small, blinds their eyes to the many things that demand gratitude. The difficulties they encounter, instead of driving them to God, the only source of their help, separate them from Him because they awaken unrest and repining.

Do we well to be thus unbelieving? Why should we be ungrateful and distrustful? Jesus is our friend; all heaven is interested in our welfare. We should not allow the perplexities and worries of everyday life to fret the mind and cloud the brow. If we do we shall always have something to vex and annoy. We should not indulge a solicitude that only frets and wears us, but does not help us to bear trials.

You may be perplexed in business; your prospects may grow darker and darker, and you may be threatened with loss; but do not become discouraged; cast your care upon God, and remain calm and cheerful. Pray for wisdom to manage your affairs with discretion, and thus prevent loss and disaster. Do all you can on your part to bring about favorable results. Jesus has promised His aid, but not apart from our effort. When, relying upon our Helper, you have done all you can, accept the result cheerfully.

It is not the will of God that His people should be weighed down with care. But our Lord does not deceive us. He does not say to us, "Do not fear; there are no dangers in your path." He knows there are trials and dangers, and He deals with us plainly. He does not propose to take His people out of a world of sin and evil, but He points them to a never-failing refuge. His prayer for His disciples was, "I pray not that Thou shouldest take them out of the world, but that Thou shouldest keep them from the evil." "In the world," He says, "ye shall have tribulation: but be of good cheer; I have overcome the world." John 17:15, 16:33.

In His Sermon on the Mount, Christ taught His disciples precious lessons in regard to the necessity of trusting in God. These lessons were designed to encourage the children of God through all ages, and they have come down to our time full of instruction and comfort. The Saviour pointed His followers to the birds of the air as they warbled their carols of praise, unencumbered with thoughts of care, for "they sow not, neither do they reap." And yet the great Father provides for their needs. The Saviour asks, "Are ye not much better than they?" Matthew 6:26. The great Provider for man and beast opens His hand and supplies all His creatures. The birds of the air are not beneath His notice. He does not drop the food into their bills, but He makes provision for their needs. They must gather the grains He has scattered for them. They must prepare the material for their little nests. They must feed their young. They go forth singing to their labor, for "your heavenly Father feedeth them." And "are ye not much better than they?" Are not you, as intelligent, spiritual worshipers, of more value than the birds of the air? Will not the Author of our being, the Preserver of our life, the One who formed us in His own divine image, provide for our necessities if we but trust in Him?

Christ pointed His disciples to the flowers of the field, growing in rich profusion and glowing in the simple beauty which the heavenly Father had given them, as an expression of His love to man. He said, "Consider the lilies of the field, how they grow." The beauty and simplicity of these natural flowers far outrival the splendor of Solomon. The most gorgeous attire produced by the skill of art cannot bear comparison with the natural grace and radiant beauty of the flowers of God's creation. Jesus asks, "If God so clothe the grass of the field, which today is, and tomorrow is cast into the oven, shall He not much more clothe you, O ye of little faith?" Matthew 6:28, 30. If God, the divine Artist, gives to the simple flowers that perish in a day their delicate and varied colors, how much greater care will He have for those who are created in His own image? This lesson of Christ's is a rebuke to the anxious thought, the perplexity and doubt, of the faithless heart.

The Lord would have all His sons and daughters happy, peaceful, and obedient. Jesus says, "My peace I give unto you: not as the world giveth, give I unto you. Let not your heart be troubled, neither let it be afraid." "These things have I spoken unto you, that My joy might remain in you, and that your joy might be full." John 14:27; 15:11.

Happiness that is sought from selfish motives, outside of the path of duty, is ill-balanced, fitful, and transitory; it passes away, and the soul is filled with loneliness and sorrow; but there is joy and satisfaction in the service of God; the Christian is not left to walk in uncertain paths; he is not left to vain regrets and disappointments. If we do not have the pleasures of this life we may still be joyful in looking to the life beyond.

But even here Christians may have the joy of communion with Christ; they may have the light of His love, the perpetual comfort of His presence. Every step in life may bring us closer to Jesus, may give us a deeper experience of His love, and may bring us one step nearer to the blessed home of peace. Then let us not cast away our confidence, but have firm assurance, firmer than ever before. "Hitherto hath the Lord helped us," and He will help us to the end. 1 Samuel 7:12. Let us look to the monumental pillars, reminders of what the Lord has done to comfort us and to save us from the hand of the destroyer. Let us keep fresh in our memory all the tender mercies that God has shown us,—the tears He has wiped away, the pains He has soothed, the anxieties removed, the fears dispelled, the wants supplied, the blessings bestowed,—thus strengthening ourselves for all that is before us through the remainder of our pilgrimage.

We cannot but look forward to new perplexities in the coming conflict, but we may look on what is past as well as on what is to come, and say, "Hitherto hath the Lord helped us." "As thy days, so shall thy strength be." Deuteronomy 33:25. The trial will not exceed the strength that shall be given us to bear it. Then let us take up our work just where we find it, believing that whatever may come, strength proportionate to the trial will be given.

And by and by the gates of heaven will be thrown open to admit God's children, and from the lips of the King of glory the benediction will fall on their ears like richest music, "Come, ye blessed of My Father, inherit the kingdom prepared for you from the foundation of the world." Matthew 25:34.

Then the redeemed will be welcomed to the home that Jesus is preparing for them. There their companions will not be the vile of earth, liars, idolaters, the impure, and unbelieving; but they will associate with those who have overcome Satan and through divine grace have formed perfect characters. Every sinful tendency, every imperfection, that afflicts them here has been removed by the blood of Christ, and the excellence and brightness of His glory, far exceeding the brightness of the sun, is imparted to them. And the moral beauty, the perfection of His character, shines through them, in worth far exceeding this outward splendor. They are without fault before the great white throne, sharing the dignity and the privileges of the angels.

In view of the glorious inheritance that may be his, "what shall a man give in exchange for his soul?" Matthew 16:26. He may be poor, yet he possesses in himself a wealth and dignity that the world could never bestow. The soul redeemed and cleansed from sin, with all its noble powers dedicated to the service of God, is of surpassing worth; and there is joy in heaven in the presence of God and the holy angels over one soul redeemed, a joy that is expressed in songs of holy triumph.

14

True and False Theories Contrasted

The sanctification set forth in the Sacred Scriptures has to do with the entire being—spirit, soul, and body. Here is the true idea of entire consecration. Paul prays that the church at Thessalonica may enjoy this great blessing. "The very God of peace sanctify you wholly; and I pray God your whole spirit and soul and body be preserved blameless unto the coming of our Lord Jesus Christ" (1 Thess. 5:23).

There is in the religious world a theory of sanctification which is false in itself and dangerous in its influence. In many cases those who profess sanctification do not possess the genuine article. Their sanctification consists in talk and will worship. Those who are really seeking to perfect Christian character will never indulge the thought that they are sinless. Their lives may be irreproachable, they may be living representatives of the truth which they have accepted; but the more they discipline their minds to dwell upon the character of Christ, and the nearer they approach to His divine image, the more clearly will they discern its spotless perfection, and the more deeply will they feel their own defects.

When persons claim that they are sanctified, they give sufficient evidence that they are far from being holy. They fail to see their own weakness and destitution. They look upon themselves as reflecting the image of Christ, because they have no true knowledge of Him. The greater the distance between them and their Saviour, the more righteous they appear in their own eyes.

While with penitence and humble trust we meditate upon Jesus, whom our sins have pierced and our sorrows have burdened, we may learn to walk in His footsteps. By beholding Him we become changed into His divine likeness. And when this work is wrought in us, we shall claim no righteousness of our own, but shall exalt Jesus Christ, while we hang our helpless souls upon His merits.

Self-righteousness Condemned

Our Saviour ever condemned self-righteousness. He taught His disciples that the highest type of religion is that which manifests itself in a quiet, unobtrusive manner. He cautioned them to perform their deeds of charity quietly; not for display, not to be praised or honored of men, but for the glory of God, expecting their reward hereafter. If they should perform good deeds to be lauded by men, no reward would be given them by their Father in heaven.

The followers of Christ were instructed not to pray for the purpose of being heard of men. "But thou, when thou prayest, enter into thy closet, and when thou hast shut thy door, pray to thy Father which is in secret; and thy Father which seeth in secret shall reward thee openly" (Matt. 6:6). Such expressions as this from the lips of Christ show that He did not regard with approval that kind of piety so prevalent among the Pharisees. His teachings upon the mount show that deeds of benevolence assume a noble form and acts of religious worship shed a most precious fragrance when performed in an unpretending manner, in penitence and humility. The pure motive sanctifies the act.

True sanctification is an entire conformity to the will of God. Rebellious thoughts and feelings are overcome, and the voice of Jesus awakens a new life, which pervades the entire being. Those who are truly sanctified will not set up their own opinion as a standard of right and wrong. They are not bigoted or self-righteous; but they are jealous of self, ever fearing lest, a promise being left them, they should come short of complying with the conditions upon which the promises are based.

Substituting Feeling for Reason

Many who profess sanctification are entirely ignorant of the work of grace upon the heart. When proved and tested, they are found to be like the self-righteous Pharisee. They will bear no contradiction. They lay aside reason and judgment, and depend wholly upon their feelings, basing their claims to sanctification upon emotions which they have at some time experienced. They are stubborn and perverse in urging their tenacious claims of holiness, giving many words, but bearing no precious fruit as proof. These professedly sanctified persons are not only deluding their own souls by their pretensions, but are exerting an influence to lead astray many who earnestly desire to conform to the will of God. They may be heard to reiterate again and again, "God leads me! God teaches me! I am living without sin!" Many who come in contact with this spirit encounter a dark, mysterious something which they cannot comprehend. But it is that which is altogether unlike Christ, the only true pattern.

Bible sanctification does not consist in strong emotion. Here is where many are led into error. They make feelings their criterion. When they feel elated or happy, they claim that they are sanctified. Happy feelings or the absence of joy is no evidence that a person is or is not sanctified. There is no such thing as instantaneous sanctification. True sanctification is a daily work, continuing as long as life shall last. Those who are battling with daily temptations, overcoming their own sinful tendencies, and seeking for holiness of heart and life, make no boastful claims of holiness. They are hungering and thirsting for righteousness. Sin appears to them exceedingly sinful.

There are those claiming sanctification who make a profession of the truth, like their brethren, and it may be difficult to make a distinction between them; but the difference exists, nevertheless. The testimony of those claiming such an exalted experience will cause the sweet Spirit of Christ to withdraw from a meeting, and will leave a chilling influence upon those present, while if they were truly living without sin, their very presence would bring holy angels into the assembly, and their words would indeed be "like apples of gold in pictures of silver" (Prov. 25:11).

The Testing Time

In summer, as we look upon the trees of the distant forest, all clothed with a beautiful mantle of green, we may not be able to distinguish between the evergreens and the other trees. But as winter approaches, and the frost king encloses them in his icy embrace, stripping the other trees of their beautiful foliage, the evergreens are readily discerned. Thus it will be with all who are walking in humility, distrustful of self, but clinging tremblingly to the hand of Christ. While those who are self-confident, and trust in their own perfection of character, lose their false robe of righteousness when subjected to the storms of trial, the truly righteous, who sincerely love and fear God, wear the robe of Christ's righteousness in prosperity and adversity alike.

Self-denial, self-sacrifice, benevolence, kindness, love, patience, fortitude, and Christian trust are the daily fruits borne by those who are truly connected with God. Their acts may not be published to the world, but they themselves are daily wrestling with evil, and gaining precious victories over temptation and wrong. Solemn vows are renewed, and kept through the strength gained by earnest prayer and constant watching thereunto. The ardent enthusiast does not discern the struggles of these silent workers; but the eye of Him who seeth the secrets of the heart, notices and regards with approval every effort put forth in lowliness and meekness. It requires the testing time to reveal the pure gold of love and faith in the character. When trials and perplexities come upon the church, then the steadfast zeal and warm affections of Christ's true followers are developed.

We feel sad to see professed Christians led astray by the false and be-witching theory that they are perfect, because it is so difficult to undeceive them and lead them into the right path. They have sought to make the exterior fair and pleasing, while the inward adorning, the meekness and lowliness of Christ, is wanting. The testing time will come to all, when the hopes of many who have for years thought themselves secure, will be seen to be without foundation. When in new positions, under varied circumstances, some who have seemed to be pillars in the house of God reveal only rotten timber be-neath the paint and varnish. But the humble in heart, who have daily felt the importance of riveting their souls to the eternal Rock, will stand unmoved amid the tempests of trial, because they trusted not to themselves. "The foundation of God standeth sure, having this seal, The Lord knoweth them that are his" (2 Tim. 2:19).

Normal Fruit Bearing

Those who take pains to call attention to their good works, constantly talking of their sinless state and endeavoring to make their religious attainments prominent, are only deceiving their own souls by so doing. A healthy man, who is able to attend to the vocations of life and who goes forth day after day to his labor with buoyant spirits and with a healthy current of blood flowing through his veins, does not call the attention of every one he meets to his soundness of body. Health and vigor are the natural conditions of his life, and therefore he is scarcely conscious that he is in the enjoyment of so rich a boon.

Thus it is with the truly righteous man. He is unconscious of his goodness and piety. Religious principle has become the spring of his life and conduct, and it is just as natural for him to bear the fruits of the Spirit as for the fig tree to bear figs or for the rosebush to yield roses. His nature is so thoroughly imbued with love for God and his fellow men that he works the works of Christ with a willing heart.

All who come within the sphere of his influence perceive the beauty and fragrance of his Christian life, while he himself is unconscious of it, for it is in harmony with his habits and inclinations. He prays for divine light, and loves to walk in that light. It is his meat and drink to do the will of his heavenly Father. His life is hid with Christ in God; yet he does not boast of this, nor seem conscious of it. God smiles upon the humble and lowly ones who follow closely in the footsteps of the Master. Angels are attracted to them, and love to linger about their path. They may be passed by as unworthy of notice by those who claim exalted attainments and who delight in making prominent their good works, but heavenly angels bend lovingly over them and are as a wall of fire round about them.

Why Christ Was Rejected

Our Saviour was the light of the world, but the world knew Him not. He was constantly employed in works of mercy, shedding light upon the pathway of all; yet He did not call upon those with whom He mingled to behold His unexampled virtue, His self-denial, self-sacrifice, and benevolence. The Jews did not admire such a life. They considered His religion worthless, because it did not accord with their standard of piety. They decided that Christ was not religious in spirit or character; for their religion consisted in display, in praying publicly, and in doing works of charity for effect. They trumpeted their good deeds, as do those who claim sanctification. They would have all understand that they are without sin. But the whole life of Christ was in direct contrast to this. He sought neither gain nor honor. His wonderful acts of healing were performed in as quiet a manner as possible, although He could not restrain the enthusiasm of those who were the recipients of His great blessings. Humility and meekness characterized His life. And it was because of His lowly walk and unassuming manners, which were in such marked contrast to their own, that the Pharisees would not accept Him.

Meekness a Fruit of the Spirit

The most precious fruit of sanctification is the grace of meekness. When this grace presides in the soul, the disposition is molded by its influence. There is a continual waiting upon God and a submission of the will to His. The understanding grasps every divine truth, and the will bows to every divine precept, without doubting or murmuring. True meekness softens and subdues the heart and gives the mind a fitness for the engrafted word. It brings the thoughts into obedience to Jesus Christ. It opens the heart to the word of God, as Lydia's was opened. It places us with Mary, as learners at the feet of Jesus. "The meek will he guide in judgment: and the meek will he teach his way" (Ps. 25:9).

The language of the meek is never that of boasting. Like the child Samuel, they pray, "Speak, Lord; for thy servant heareth" (1 Sam. 3:9). When Joshua was placed in the highest position of honor, as commander of Israel, he bade defiance to all the enemies of God. His heart was filled with noble thoughts of his great mission. Yet upon the intimation of a message from Heaven he placed himself in the position of a little child to be directed. "What saith my lord unto his servant?" (Joshua 5:14), was his response. The first words of Paul after Christ was revealed to him were, "Lord, what wilt thou have me to do?" (Acts 9:6).

Meekness in the school of Christ is one of the marked fruits of the Spirit. It is a grace wrought by the Holy Spirit as a sanctifier, and enables its possessor at all times to control a rash and impetuous temper. When the grace of meekness is cherished by those who are naturally sour or hasty in disposition, they will put forth the most earnest efforts to subdue their unhappy temper. Every day they will gain self-control, until that which is unlovely and unlike Jesus is conquered. They become assimilated to the Divine Pattern, until they can obey the inspired injunction, "Be swift to hear, slow to speak, slow to wrath" (James 1:19).

When a man professes to be sanctified, and yet in words and works may be represented by the impure fountain sending forth its bitter waters, we may safely say, That man is deceived. He needs to learn the very alphabet of what constitutes the life of a Christian. Some who profess to be servants of Christ have so long cherished the demon of unkindness that they seem to love the unhallowed element and to take pleasure in speaking words that displease and irritate. These men must be converted before Christ will acknowledge them as His children.

Meekness is the inward adorning, which God estimates as of great price. The apostle speaks of this as more excellent and valuable than gold or pearls or costly array. While the outward adorning beautifies only the mortal body, the ornament of meekness adorns the soul and connects finite man with the infinite God. This is the ornament of God's own choice. He who garnished the heavens with the orbs of light has by the same Spirit promised that "he will beautify the meek with salvation" (Ps. 149:4). Angels of heaven will register as best adorned those who put on the Lord Jesus Christ and walk with Him in meekness and lowliness of mind.

There are high attainments for the Christian. He may ever be rising to higher attainments. John had an elevated idea of the privilege of a Christian. He says, "Behold, what manner of love the Father hath bestowed upon us, that we should be called the sons of God" (1 John 3:1). It is not possible for humanity to rise to a higher dignity than is here implied. To man is granted the privilege of becoming an heir of God and a joint heir with Christ. To those who have been thus exalted, are unfolded the unsearchable riches of Christ, which are of a thousandfold more value than the wealth of the world. Thus, through the merits of Jesus Christ, finite man is elevated to fellowship with God and with His dear Son.

15

Daniel's Temperance Principles

The prophet Daniel was an illustrious character. He was a bright example of what men may become when united with the God of wisdom. A brief account of the life of this holy man of God is left on record for the encouragement of those who should afterward be called to endure trial and temptation.

When the people of Israel, their king, nobles, and priests were carried into captivity, four of their number were selected to serve in the court of the king of Babylon. One of these was Daniel, who early gave promise of the remarkable ability developed in later years. These youth were all of princely birth, and are described as "children in whom was no blemish, but well favoured, and skilful in all wisdom, and cunning in knowledge, and understanding science, and such as had ability in them" (Dan. 1:4). Perceiving the superior talents of these youthful captives, King Nebuchadnezzar determined to prepare them to fill important positions in his kingdom. That they might be fully qualified for their life at court, according to Oriental custom, they were to be taught the language of the Chaldeans, and to be subjected for three years to a thorough course of physical and intellectual discipline.

The youth in this school of training were not only to be admitted to the royal palace, but it was provided that they should eat of the meat and drink of the wine which came from the king's table. In all this the king considered that he was not only bestowing great honor upon them, but securing for them the best physical and mental development that could be attained.

Meeting the Test

Among the viands placed before the king were swine's flesh and other meats which were declared unclean by the law of Moses, and which the Hebrews had been expressly forbidden to eat. Here Daniel was brought to a severe test. Should he adhere to the teachings of his fathers concerning meats and drinks, and offend the king, and probably lose not only his position but his life? or should he disregard the commandment of the Lord, and retain the favor of the king, thus securing great intellectual advantages and the most flattering worldly prospects?

Daniel did not long hesitate. He decided to stand firm in his integrity, let the result be what it might. He "purposed in his heart that he would not defile himself with the portion of the king's meat, nor with the wine which he drank" (Dan. 1:8).

Not Narrow or Bigoted

There are many among professed Christians today who would decide that Daniel was too particular, and would pronounce him narrow and bigoted. They consider the matter of eating and drinking as of too little consequence to require such a decided stand—one involving the probable sacrifice of every earthly advantage. But those who reason thus will find in the day of judgment that they turned from God's express requirements and set up their own opinion as a standard of right and wrong. They will find that what seemed to them unimportant was not so regarded of God. His requirements should be sacredly obeyed. Those who accept and obey one of His precepts because it is convenient to do so, while they reject another because its observance would require a sacrifice, lower the standard of right and by their example lead others to lightly regard the holy law of God. "Thus saith the Lord" is to be our rule in all things.

A Faultless Character

Daniel was subjected to the severest temptations that can assail the youth of today; yet he was true to the religious instruction received in early life. He was surrounded with influences calculated to subvert those who would vacillate between principle and inclination; yet the Word of God presents him as a faultless character. Daniel dared not trust to his own moral power. Prayer was to him a necessity. He made God his strength, and the fear of God was continually before him in all the transactions of his life.

Daniel possessed the grace of genuine meekness. He was true, firm, and noble. He sought to live in peace with all, while he was unbending as the lofty cedar wherever principle was involved. In everything that did not come in collision with his allegiance to God, he was respectful and obedient to those who had authority over him; but he had so high a sense of the claims of God that the requirements of earthly rulers were held subordinate. He would not be induced by any selfish consideration to swerve from his duty.

The character of Daniel is presented to the world as a striking example of what God's grace can make of men fallen by nature and corrupted by sin. The record of his noble, self-denying life is an encouragement to our common humanity. From it we may gather strength to nobly resist temptation, and firmly, and in the grace of meekness, stand for the right under the severest trial.

God's Approval Dearer Than Life

Daniel might have found a plausible excuse to depart from his strictly temperate habits; but the approval of God was dearer to him than the favor of the most powerful earthly potentate—dearer even than life itself. Having by his courteous conduct obtained favor with Melzar, the officer in charge of the

Hebrew youth, Daniel made a request that they might not eat of the king's meat or drink of his wine. Melzar feared that should he comply with this request, he might incur the displeasure of the king, and thus endanger his own life. Like many at the present day, he thought that an abstemious diet would render these youth pale and sickly in appearance and deficient in muscular strength, while the luxurious food from the king's table would make them ruddy and beautiful and would promote physical and mental activity.

Daniel requested that the matter be decided by a ten days' trial—the Hebrew youth during this brief period being permitted to eat of simple food, while their companions partook of the king's dainties. The request was finally granted, and then Daniel felt assured that he had gained his case. Although but a youth, he had seen the injurious effects of wine and luxurious living upon physical and mental health.

God Vindicates His Servant

At the end of the ten days the result was found to be quite the opposite of Melzar's expectations. Not only in personal appearance, but in physical activity and mental vigor, those who had been temperate in their habits exhibited a marked superiority over their companions who had indulged appetite. As a result of this trial, Daniel and his associates were permitted to continue their simple diet during the whole course of their training for the duties of the kingdom.

The Lord regarded with approval the firmness and self-denial of these Hebrew youth, and His blessing attended them. He "gave them knowledge and skill in all learning and wisdom: and Daniel had understanding in all visions and dreams" (Dan. 1:17). At the expiration of the three years of training, when their ability and acquirements were tested by the king, he "found none like Daniel, Hananiah, Mishael, and Azariah: therefore stood they before the king. And in all matters of wisdom and understanding, that the king enquired of them, he found them ten times better than all the magicians and astrologers that were in all his realm" (verse 20).

Self-control a Condition of Sanctification

The life of Daniel is an inspired illustration of what constitutes a sanctified character. It presents a lesson for all, and especially for the young. A strict compliance with the requirements of God is beneficial to the health of body and mind. In order to reach the highest standard of moral and intellectual attainments, it is necessary to seek wisdom and strength from God and to observe strict temperance in all the habits of life. In the experience of Daniel and his companions we have an instance of the triumph of principle over temptation to indulge the appetite. It shows us that through religious principle young men may triumph over the lusts of the flesh and remain true to God's requirements, even though it cost them a great sacrifice.

What if Daniel and his companions had made a compromise with those heathen officers and had yielded to the pressure of the occasion by eating and drinking as was customary with the Babylonians? That single instance of departure from principle would have weakened their sense of right and their abhorrence of wrong. Indulgence of appetite would have involved the sacrifice of physical vigor, clearness of intellect, and spiritual power. One wrong step would probably have led to others, until, their connection with Heaven being severed, they would have been swept away by temptation.

God has said, "Them that honour me I will honour" (1 Sam. 2:30). While Daniel clung to his God with unwavering trust, the Spirit of prophetic power came upon him. While he was instructed of man in the duties of court life, he was taught of God to read the mysteries of future ages and to present to coming generations, through figures and similitudes, the wonderful things that would come to pass in the last days.

16

Controlling the Appetites and Passions

Abstain from fleshy lusts, which war against the soul," is the language of the apostle Peter (1 Peter 2:11). Many regard this text as a warning against licentiousness only, but it has a broader meaning. It forbids every injurious gratification of appetite or passion. Let none who profess godliness regard with indifference the health of the body, and flatter themselves that intemperance is no sin, and will not affect their spirituality. A close sympathy exists between the physical and the moral nature. Any habit which does not promote health degrades the higher and nobler faculties. Wrong habits of eating and drinking lead to errors in thought and action. Indulgence of appetite strengthens the animal propensities, giving them the ascendancy over the mental and spiritual powers.

It is impossible for any to enjoy the blessing of sanctification while they are selfish and gluttonous. Many groan under a burden of infirmities because of wrong habits of eating and drinking, which do violence to the laws of life and health. They are enfeebling their digestive organs by indulging perverted appetite. The power of the human constitution to resist the abuses put upon it is wonderful, but persistent wrong habits in excessive eating and drinking will enfeeble every function of the body. In the gratification of perverted appetite and passion even professed Christians cripple nature in her work and lessen physical, mental, and moral power. Let these feeble ones consider what they might have been had thy lived temperately and promoted health instead of abusing it.

Not an Impossible Standard

When Paul wrote, "The very God of peace sanctify you wholly" (1 Thess. 5:23), he did not exhort his brethren to aim at a standard which it was impossible for them to reach; he did not pray that they might have blessings which it was not the will of God to give. He knew that all who would be fitted to meet Christ in peace must possess a pure and holy character. "Every man that striveth for the mastery is temperate in all things. Now they do it to obtain a corruptible crown; but we an incorruptible. I therefore so run, not as uncertainly; so fight I, not as one that beateth the air: but I keep under my body, and bring it into subjection: lest that by any means, when I have preached to others, I myself should be a castaway" (1 Cor. 9:25-27). "What? know ye not that your body is the temple of the Holy Ghost which is in you, which ye have of God, and ye are not your own? For ye are bought with a price: therefore glorify God in your body, and in your spirit, which are God's" (1 Cor. 6:19, 20).

An Unblemished Offering

Again, the apostle writes to the believers, "I beseech you therefore, brethren, by the mercies of God, that ye present your bodies a living sacrifice, holy, acceptable unto God, which is your reasonable service" (Rom. 12: 1). Specific directions were given to ancient Israel that no defective or diseased animal should be presented as an offering to God. Only the most perfect were to be selected for this purpose. The Lord, through the prophet Malachi, most severely reproved His people for departing from these instructions.

"A son honoureth his father, and a servant his master: if then I be a father, where is mine honour? and if I be a master, where is my fear? saith the Lord of hosts unto you, O priests, that despise my name. And ye say, Wherein have we despised thy name? Ye offer polluted bread upon mine altar; and ye say, Wherein have we polluted thee? In that ye say, The table of the Lord is contemptible. And if ye offer the blind for sacrifice, is it not evil? and if ye offer the lame and sick, is it not evil? offer it now unto thy governor; will he be pleased with thee, or accept thy person? saith the Lord of hosts. . . . Ye brought that which was torn, and the lame, and the sick; thus ye brought an offering: should I accept this of your hand? saith the Lord" (Mal. 1:6-13).

Though addressed to ancient Israel, these words contain a lesson for the people of God today. When the apostle appeals to his brethren to present their bodies "a living sacrifice, holy, acceptable unto God," he sets forth the principles of true sanctification. It is not merely a theory, an emotion, or a form of words, but a living, active principle, entering into the everyday life. It requires that our habits of eating, drinking, and dressing be such as to secure the preservation of physical, mental, and moral health, that we may present to the Lord our bodies, not an offering corrupted by wrong habits, but "a living sacrifice, holy, acceptable unto God."

Stimulants and Narcotics

Peter's admonition to abstain from fleshly lusts is a most direct and forcible warning against the use of all such stimulants and narcotics as tea, coffee, tobacco, alcohol, and morphine. These indulgences may well be classed among the lusts that exert a pernicious influence upon moral character. The earlier these hurtful habits are formed, the more firmly will they hold their victim in slavery to lust, and the more certainly will they lower the standard of spirituality.

Bible teaching will make but a feeble impression upon those whose faculties are benumbed by self-gratification. Thousands will sacrifice not only health and life but their hope of heaven before they will wage war against their own perverted appetites. One lady who for many years claimed to be sanctified, made the statement that if she must give up her pipe or heaven she would say, "Farewell, heaven; I cannot overcome my love for my pipe." This idol had been enshrined in the soul, leaving to Jesus a subordinate place.

Yet this woman claimed to be wholly the Lord's!

Lusts That War Against the Soul

Wherever they may be, those who are truly sanctified will elevate the moral standard by preserving correct physical habits, and, like Daniel, presenting to others an example of temperance and self-denial. Every depraved appetite becomes a warring lust. Everything that conflicts with natural law creates a diseased condition of the soul. The indulgence of appetite produces a dyspeptic stomach, a torpid liver, a clouded brain, and thus perverts the temper and spirit of the man. And these enfeebled powers are offered to God, who refused to accept the victims for sacrifice unless they were without a blemish! It is our duty to bring our appetites and our habits of life into conformity to natural law. If the bodies offered upon Christ's altar were examined with the close scrutiny to which the Jewish sacrifices were subjected, who would be accepted?

With what care should Christians regulate their habits, that they may preserve the full vigor of every faculty to give to the service of Christ. If we would be sanctified, in soul, body, and spirit, we must live in conformity to the divine law. The heart cannot preserve consecration to God while the appetites and passions are indulged at the expense of health and life. Those who violate the laws upon which health depends, must suffer the penalty. They have so limited their abilities in every sense that they cannot properly discharge their duties to their fellow men, and they utterly fail to answer the claims of God.

When Lord Palmerston, premier of England, was petitioned by the Scotch clergy to appoint a day of fasting and prayer to avert the cholera, he replied, in effect, "Cleanse and disinfect your streets and houses, promote cleanliness and health among the poor, and see that they are plentifully supplied with good food and raiment, and employ right sanitary measures generally, and you will have no occasion to fast and pray. Nor will the Lord hear your prayers while these, His preventives, remain unheeded."

Says Paul, "Let us cleanse ourselves from all filthiness of the flesh and spirit, perfecting holiness in the fear of God" (2 Cor. 7:1). He presents for our encouragement the freedom enjoyed by the truly sanctified: "There is therefore now no condemnation to them which are in Christ Jesus, who walk not after the flesh, but after the Spirit" (Rom. 8:1). He charges the Galatians, "Walk in the Spirit, and ye shall not fulfil the lust of the flesh" (Gal. 5:16). He names some of the forms of fleshly lust—"idolatry, . . . drunkenness, . . . and such like" (verses 20, 21). And after mentioning the fruits of the Spirit, among which is temperance, he adds, "And they that are Christ's have crucified the flesh with the affections and lusts" (verse 24).

Tobacco

James says that the wisdom which is from above is "first pure" (James

3:17). If he had seen his brethren using tobacco, would he not have denounced the practice as "earthly, sensual, devilish" (verse 15)? In this age of Christian light, how often the lips that take the precious name of Christ are defiled by tobacco spittle and the breath is polluted with the stench. Surely, the soul that can enjoy such uncleanness must also be defiled. As I have seen men who claimed to enjoy the blessing of entire sanctification, while they were slaves to tobacco, polluting everything around them, I have thought, How would heaven appear with tobacco users in it? God's word has plainly declared that "there shall in no wise enter into it any thing that defileth" (Rev. 21:27). How, then, can those who indulge this filthy habit hope to find admittance there?

Men professing godliness offer their bodies upon Satan's altar and burn the incense of tobacco to his satanic majesty. Does this statement seem severe? Certainly, the offering is presented to some deity. As God is pure and holy, and will accept nothing defiling in its character, He must refuse this expensive, filthy, and unholy sacrifice; therefore we conclude that Satan is the one who claims the honor.

Jesus died to rescue man from the grasp of Satan. He came to set us free by the blood of His atoning sacrifice. The man who has become the property of Jesus Christ, and whose body is the temple of the Holy Ghost, will not be enslaved by the pernicious habit of tobacco using. His powers belong to Christ, who has bought him with the price of blood. His property is the Lord's. How, then, can he be guiltless in expending every day the Lord's entrusted capital to gratify an appetite which has no foundation in nature?

An enormous sum is yearly squandered for this indulgence, while souls are perishing for the word of life. Professed Christians rob God in tithes and offerings, while they offer on the altar of destroying lust, in the use of tobacco, more than they give to relieve the poor or to supply the wants of God's cause. Those who are truly sanctified will overcome every hurtful lust. Then all these channels of needless expense will be turned to the Lord's treasury, and Christians will take the lead in self-denial, in self-sacrifice, and in temperance. Then they will be the light of the world.

Tea and Coffee

Tea and coffee, as well as tobacco, have an injurious effect upon the system. Tea is intoxicating. Though less in degree, its effect is the same in character as that of spirituous liquors. Coffee has a greater tendency to becloud the intellect and benumb the energies. It is not so powerful as tobacco, but is similar in its effects. The arguments brought against tobacco may also be urged against the use of tea and coffee.

When those who are in the habit of using tea, coffee, tobacco, opium, or spirituous liquors are deprived of the accustomed indulgence, they find it impossible to engage with interest and zeal in the worship of God. Divine grace seems powerless to enliven or spiritualize their prayers or their testimonies.

These professed Christians should consider the source of their enjoyment. Is it from above, or from beneath?

To a user of stimulants, everything seems insipid without the darling indulgence. This deadens the natural sensibilities of both body and mind and renders him less susceptible to the influence of the Holy Spirit. In the absence of the usual stimulant he has a hungering of body and soul, not for righteousness, not for holiness, not for God's presence, but for his cherished idol. In the indulgence of hurtful lusts, professed Christians are daily enfeebling their powers, making it impossible to glorify God.

17

The Fiery Furnace

In the same year that Daniel and his companions entered the service of the king of Babylon events occurred that severely tested the integrity of these youthful Hebrews and proved before an idolatrous nation the power and faithfulness of the God of Israel.

While King Nebuchadnezzar was looking forward with anxious forebodings to the future, he had a remarkable dream, by which he was greatly troubled, "and his sleep brake from him" (Dan. 2:1). But although this vision of the night made a deep impression on his mind, he found it impossible to recall the particulars. He applied to his astrologers and magicians, and with promises of great wealth and honor commanded them to tell him his dream and its interpretation. But they said, "Tell thy servants the dream, and we will shew the interpretation" (verse 4).

The king knew that if they could really tell the interpretation, they could tell the dream as well. The Lord had in His providence given Nebuchadnezzar this dream, and had caused the particulars to be forgotten, while the fearful impression was left upon his mind, in order to expose the pretensions of the wise men of Babylon. The monarch was very angry, and threatened that they should all be slain if, in a given time, the dream was not made known. Daniel and his companions were to perish with the false prophets; but, taking his life in his hand, Daniel ventures to enter the presence of the king, begging that time may be granted that he may show the dream and the interpretation.

To this request the monarch accedes; and now Daniel gathers his three companions, and together they take the matter before God, seeking for wisdom from the Source of light and knowledge. Although they were in the king's court, surrounded with temptation, they did not forget their responsibility to God. They were strong in the consciousness that His providence had placed them where they were; that they were doing His work, meeting the demands of truth and duty. They had confidence toward God. They had turned to Him for strength when in perplexity and danger, and He had been to them an ever-present help.

The Secret Revealed

The servants of God did not plead with Him in vain. They had honored Him, and in the hour of trial He honored them. The secret was revealed to Daniel, and he hastened to request an interview with the king.

The Jewish captive stands before the monarch of the most powerful empire the sun has ever shone upon. The king is in great distress amid all his riches and glory, but the youthful exile is peaceful and happy in his God. Now, if ever, is the time for Daniel to exalt himself, to make prominent his own goodness and superior wisdom. But his first effort is to disclaim all honor for himself and to exalt God as the source of wisdom:

"The secret which the king hath demanded cannot the wise men, the astrologers, the magicians, the soothsayers, shew unto the king; but there is a God in heaven that revealeth secrets, and maketh known to the king Nebuchadnezzar what shall be in the latter days" (Dan. 2:27, 28). The king listens with solemn attention as every particular of the dream is reproduced; and when the interpretation is faithfully given, he feels that he can rely upon it as a divine revelation.

The solemn truths conveyed in this vision of the night made a deep impression on the sovereign's mind, and in humility and awe he fell down and worshiped, saying, "Of a truth it is, that your God is a God of gods, and a Lord of kings, and a revealer of secrets" (verse 47).

The Golden Image

Light direct from Heaven had been permitted to shine upon King Nebuchadnezzar, and for a little time he was influenced by the fear of God. But a few years of prosperity filled his heart with pride, and he forgot his acknowledgment of the living God. He resumed his idol worship with increased zeal and bigotry.

From the treasures obtained in war he made a golden image to represent the one that he had seen in his dream, setting it up in the plain of Dura, and commanding all the rulers and the people to worship it, on pain of death. This statue was about ninety feet in height and nine in breadth, and in the eyes of that idolatrous people it presented a most imposing and majestic appearance. A proclamation was issued calling upon all the officers of the kingdom to assemble at the dedication of the image, and at the sound of the musical instruments, to bow down and worship it. Should any fail to do this, they were immediately to be cast into the midst of a burning fiery furnace.

The appointed day has come, and the vast company is assembled, when word is brought to the king that the three Hebrews whom he has set over the province of Babylon have refused to worship the image. These are Daniel's three companions, who had been called by the king, Shadrach, Meshach, and Abednego. Full of rage, the monarch calls them before him, and pointing to the angry furnace, tells them the punishment that will be theirs if they refuse obedience to his will.

In vain were the king's threats. He could not turn these noble men from their allegiance to the great Ruler of nations. They had learned from the history of their fathers that disobedience to God is dishonor, disaster, and ruin; that the fear of the Lord is not only the beginning of wisdom but the foundation of all true prosperity. They look with calmness upon the fiery furnace and the idolatrous throng. They have trusted in God, and He will not fail them now. Their answer is respectful, but decided: "Be it known unto thee, O king, that we will not serve thy gods, nor worship the golden image which thou hast set up" (Dan. 3:18).

The proud monarch is surrounded by his great men, the officers of the government, and the army that has conquered nations; and all unite in applauding him as having the wisdom and power of the gods. In the midst of this imposing display stand the three youthful Hebrews, steadily persisting in their refusal to obey the king's decree. They had been obedient to the laws of Babylon so far as these did not conflict with the claims of God, but they would not be swayed a hair's breadth from the duty they owed to their Creator.

The king's wrath knew no limits. In the very height of his power and glory, to be thus defied by the representatives of a despised and captive race was an insult which his proud spirit could not endure. The fiery furnace had been heated seven times more than it was wont, and into it were cast the Hebrew exiles. So furious were the flames, that the men who cast them in were burned to death.

In the Presence of the Infinite

Suddenly the countenance of the king paled with terror. His eyes were fixed upon the glowing flames, and turning to his lords, he said, "Did not we cast three men bound into the midst of the fire?" (verse 24). The answer was, "True, O king." And now the monarch exclaimed, "Lo, I see four men loose, walking in the midst of the fire, and they have no hurt; and the form of the fourth is like the Son of God" (verse 25).

When Christ manifests Himself to the children of men, an unseen power speaks to their souls. They feel themselves to be in the presence of the Infinite One. Before His majesty, kings and nobles tremble, and acknowledge that the living God is above every earthly power.

With feelings of remorse and shame, the king exclaimed, "Ye servants of the most high God, come forth" (verse 26). And they obeyed, showing themselves unhurt before that vast multitude, not even the smell of fire being upon their garments. This miracle produced a striking change in the minds of the people. The great golden image, set up with such display, was forgotten. The king published a decree that any one speaking against the God of these men should be put to death, "because there is no other God that can deliver after this sort" (verse 29).

Steadfast Integrity and the Sanctified Life

These three Hebrews possessed genuine sanctification. True Christian principle will not stop to weigh consequences. It does not ask, What will people think of me if I do this? or, How will it affect my worldly prospects if I do that? With the most intense longing the children of God desire to know what

He would have them do, that their works may glorify Him. The Lord has made ample provision that the hearts and lives of all His followers may be controlled by divine grace, that they may be as burning and shining lights in the world.

These faithful Hebrews possessed great natural ability, they had enjoyed the highest intellectual culture, and now occupied a position of honor; but all this did not lead them to forget God. Their powers were yielded to the sanctifying influence of divine grace. By their steadfast integrity they showed forth the praises of Him who had called them out of darkness into His marvelous light. In their wonderful deliverance were displayed, before that vast assembly, the power and majesty of God. Jesus placed Himself by their side in the fiery furnace, and by the glory of His presence convinced the proud king of Babylon that it could be no other than the Son of God. The light of Heaven had been shining forth from Daniel and his companions, until all their associates understood the faith which ennobled their lives and beautified their characters. By the deliverance of His faithful servants, the Lord declares that He will take His stand with the oppressed and overthrow all earthly powers that would trample upon the authority of the God of heaven.

A Lesson to the Fainthearted

What a lesson is here given to the fainthearted, the vacillating, the cowardly in the cause of God! What encouragement to those who will not be turned aside from duty by threats or peril! These faithful, steadfast characters exemplify sanctification, while they have no thought of claiming the high honor. The amount of good which may be accomplished by comparatively obscure but devoted Christians cannot be estimated until the life records shall be made known, when the judgment shall sit and the books be opened.

Christ identifies His interest with this class; He is not ashamed to call them brethren. There should be hundreds where there is now one among us, so closely allied to God, their lives in such close conformity to His will, that they would be bright and shining lights, sanctified wholly, in soul, body, and spirit.

The conflict still goes on between the children of light and the children of darkness. Those who name the name of Christ should shake off the lethargy that enfeebles their efforts, and should meet the momentous responsibilities that devolve upon them. All who do this may expect the power of God to be revealed in them. The Son of God, the world's Redeemer, will be represented in their words and in their works, and God's name will be glorified.

As in the days of Shadrach, Meshach, and Abednego, so in the closing period of earth's history the Lord will work mightily in behalf of those who stand steadfastly for the right. He who walked with the Hebrew worthies in the fiery furnace will be with His followers wherever they are. His abiding presence will comfort and sustain. In the midst of the time of trouble—trouble such as has not been since there was a nation—His chosen ones will stand unmoved. Satan with all the hosts of evil cannot destroy the weakest of God's saints. Angels that excel in strength will protect them, and in their behalf Jehovah will reveal Himself as a "God of gods," able to save to the uttermost those who have put their trust in Him.— *Prophets and Kings*, p. 513.

18

Daniel in the Lions' Den

When Darius took possession of the throne of Babylon, he at once proceeded to reorganize the government. He "set over the kingdom an hundred and twenty princes . . . ; and over these three presidents; of whom Daniel was first" (Dan. 6:1, 2). And "Daniel was preferred above the presidents and princes, because an excellent spirit was in him; and the king thought to set him over the whole realm" (verse 3). The honors bestowed upon Daniel excited the jealousy of the leading men of the kingdom. The presidents and princes sought to find occasion for complaint against him. "But they could find none occasion nor fault; forasmuch as he was faithful, neither was there any error or fault found in him" (verse 4).

What a lesson is here presented for all Christians. The keen eyes of jealousy were fixed upon Daniel day after day; their watchings were sharpened by hatred; yet not a word or act of his life could they make appear wrong. And still he made no claim to sanctification, but he did that which was infinitely better—he lived a life of faithfulness and consecration.

The more blameless the conduct of Daniel, the greater was the hatred excited against him by his enemies. They were filled with madness, because they could find nothing in his moral character or in the discharge of his duties upon which to base a complaint against him. "Then said these men, We shall not find any occasion against this Daniel, except we find it against him concerning the law of his God" (verse 5). Three times a day Daniel prayed to the God of heaven. This was the only accusation that could be brought against him.

A scheme was now devised to accomplish his destruction. His enemies assembled at the palace and besought the king to pass a decree that no person in the whole realm should ask anything of either God or man, except of Darius the king, for the space of thirty days, and that any violation of this edict should be punished by casting the offender into the den of lions. The king knew nothing of the hatred of these men toward Daniel, and did not suspect that the decree would in any way injure him. Through flattery they made the monarch believe it would be greatly to his honor to pass such an edict. With a smile of satanic triumph upon their faces, they come forth from the presence of the king, and rejoice together over the snare which they have laid for the servant of God.

An Example of Boldness and Fidelity

The decree goes forth from the king. Daniel is acquainted with the purpose of his enemies to ruin him. But he does not change his course in a single particular. With calmness he performs his accustomed duties, and at the hour of prayer he goes to his chamber, and with his windows open toward Jerusalem, he offers his petitions to the God of heaven. By his course of action he fearlessly declares that no earthly power has the right to come between him and his God and tell him to whom he should or should not pray. Noble man of principle! he stands before the world today a praiseworthy example of Christian boldness and fidelity. He turns to God with all his heart, although he knows that death is the penalty for his devotion.

His adversaries watch him an entire day. Three times he has repaired to his chamber, and three times the voice of earnest intercession has been heard. The next morning the complaint is made to the king that Daniel, one of the captives of Judah, has set at defiance his decree. When the monarch heard these words, his eyes were at once opened to see the snare that had been set. He was sorely displeased with himself for having passed such a decree, and labored till the going down of the sun to devise a plan by which Daniel might be delivered. But the prophet's enemies had anticipated this, and they came before the king with these words: "Know, O king, that the law of the Medes and Persians is, That no decree nor statute which the king establisheth may be changed.

"Then the king commanded, and they brought Daniel, and cast him into the den of lions. Now the king spake and said unto Daniel, Thy God whom thou servest continually, he will deliver thee" (verses 15, 16). A stone was laid upon the mouth of the den, and sealed with the royal seal. "Then the king went to his palace, and passed the night fasting: neither were instruments of musick brought before him: and his sleep went from him" (verse 18).

"My God Hath Sent His Angel"

Early in the morning the monarch hastened to the den of lions, and cried, "Daniel, Oh Daniel, servant of the living God, is thy God, whom thou servest continually, able to deliver thee from the lions?" (verse 20). The voice of the prophet was heard in reply, "Oh king, live for ever. My God hath sent his angel, and hath shut the lions' mouths, that they have not hurt me: forasmuch as before him innocency was found in me; and also before thee, Oh king, have I done no hurt.

"Then was the king exceeding glad for him, and commanded that they should take Daniel up out of the den. So Daniel was taken up out of the den, and no manner of hurt was found upon him, because he believed in his God" (verses 22, 23). Thus was the servant of God delivered. And the snare which his enemies had laid for his destruction proved to be their own ruin. At the command of the king they were cast into the den, and instantly devoured by the wild beasts.

19

Daniel's Prayers

As the time approached for the close of the seventy years' captivity, Daniel's mind became greatly exercised upon the prophecies of Jeremiah. He saw that the time was at hand when God would give His chosen people another trial; and with fasting, humiliation, and prayer, he importuned the God of heaven in behalf of Israel, in these words: "Oh Lord, the great and dreadful God, keeping the covenant and mercy to them that love him, and to them that keep his commandments; we have sinned, and have committed iniquity, and have done wickedly, and have rebelled, even by departing from thy precepts and from thy judgments; neither have we hearkened unto thy servants the prophets, which spake in thy name to our kings, our princes, and our fathers, and to all the people of the land" (Dan. 9:4-6).

Daniel does not proclaim his own fidelity before the Lord. Instead of claiming to be pure and holy, this honored prophet humbly identifies himself with the really sinful of Israel. The wisdom which God had imparted to him was as far superior to the wisdom of the great men of the world as the light of the sun shining in the heavens at noonday is brighter than the feeblest star. Yet ponder the prayer from the lips of this man so highly favored of Heaven. With deep humiliation, with tears and rending of heart, he pleads for himself and for his people. He lays his soul open before God, confessing his own unworthiness and acknowledging the Lord's greatness and majesty.

Earnestness and Fervor

What earnestness and fervor characterize his supplications! The hand of faith is reached upward to grasp the never-failing promises of the Most High. His soul is wrestling in agony. And he has the evidence that his prayer is heard. He knows that victory is his. If we as a people would pray as Daniel prayed, and wrestle as he wrestled, humbling our souls before God, we should realize as marked answers to our petitions as were granted to Daniel. Hear how he presses his case at the court of heaven:

"Oh my God, incline thine ear, and hear; open thine eyes, and behold our desolations, and the city which is called by thy name; for we do not present our supplications before thee for our righteousnesses, but for thy great mercies. Oh Lord, hear; Oh Lord, forgive; Oh Lord, hearken and do; defer not; for thine own sake, Oh my God: for thy city and thy people are called by thy name" (verses 18, 19).

The man of God was praying for the blessing of Heaven upon his people and for a clearer knowledge of the divine will. The burden of his heart was for Israel, who were not, in the strictest sense, keeping the law of God. He acknowledges that all their misfortunes have come upon them in consequence of their transgressions of that holy law. He says, "We have sinned, we have done wickedly. . . . Because for our sins, and for the iniquities of our fathers, Jerusalem and thy people are become a reproach to all that are about us" (verses 15, 16). The Jews had lost their peculiar, holy character as God's chosen people. "Now therefore, O our God, hear the prayer of thy servant, and his supplications, and cause thy face to shine upon thy sanctuary that is desolate" (verse 17). Daniel's heart turns with intense longing to the desolate sanctuary of God. He knows that its prosperity can be restored only as Israel shall repent of their transgressions of God's law, and become humble, faithful, and obedient.

The Heavenly Messenger

As Daniel's prayer is going forth, the angel Gabriel comes sweeping down from the heavenly courts to tell him that his petitions are heard and answered. This mighty angel has been commissioned to give him skill and understanding—to open before him the mysteries of future ages. Thus, while earnestly seeking to know and understand the truth, Daniel was brought into communion with Heaven's delegated messenger.

In answer to his petition, Daniel received not only the light and truth which he and his people most needed, but a view of the great events of the future, even to the advent of the world's Redeemer. Those who claim to be sanctified, while they have no desire to search the Scriptures or to wrestle with God in prayer for a clearer understanding of Bible truth, know not what true sanctification is.

Daniel talked with God. Heaven was opened before him. But the high honors granted him were the result of humiliation and earnest seeking. All who believe with the heart the word of God will hunger and thirst for a knowledge of His will. God is the author of truth. He enlightens the darkened understanding and gives to the human mind power to grasp and comprehend the truths which He has revealed.

Seeking Wisdom From God

Upon the occasion just described, the angel Gabriel imparted to Daniel all the instruction which he was then able to receive. A few years afterward, however, the prophet desired to learn more of subjects not yet fully explained, and again set himself to seek light and wisdom from God. "In those days I Daniel was mourning three full weeks. I ate no pleasant bread, neither came flesh nor wine in my mouth, neither did I anoint myself at all. . . . Then I lifted up mine eyes, and looked, and behold a certain man clothed in linen, whose loins were girded with fine gold of Uphaz. His body also was like the beryl, and his face as the appearance of lightning, and his eyes as lamps of fire, and his arms and his feet like in colour to polished brass, and the voice of his words like the voice of a multitude" (Dan. 10:2-6).

This description is similar to that given by John when Christ was revealed to him upon the Isle of Patmos. No less a personage than the Son of God appeared to Daniel. Our Lord comes with another heavenly messenger to teach Daniel what would take place in the latter days.

The great truths revealed by the world's Redeemer are for those who search for truth as for hid treasures. Daniel was an aged man. His life had been passed amid the fascinations of a heathen court, his mind cumbered with the affairs of a great empire. Yet he turns aside from all these to afflict his soul before God, and seek a knowledge of the purposes of the Most High. And in response to his supplications, light from the heavenly courts was communicated for those who should live in the latter days. With what earnestness, then, should we seek God, that He may open our understanding to comprehend the truths brought to us from heaven.

"I Daniel alone saw the vision: for the men that were with me saw not the vision; but a great quaking fell upon them, so that they fled to hide themselves. . . . And there remained no strength in me: for my comeliness was turned in me into corruption, and I retained no strength" (verses 7, 8). All who are truly sanctified will have a similar experience. The clearer their views of the greatness, glory, and perfection of Christ, the more vividly will they see their own weakness and imperfection. They will have no disposition to claim a sinless character; that which has appeared right and comely in themselves will, in contrast with Christ's purity and glory, appear only as unworthy and corruptible. It is when men are separated from God, when they have very indistinct views of Christ, that they say, "I am sinless; I am sanctified."

Gabriel now appeared to the prophet, and thus addressed him: "Oh Daniel, a man greatly beloved, understand the words that I speak unto thee, and stand upright: for unto thee am I now sent. And when he had spoken this word unto me, I stood trembling. Then said he unto me, Fear not, Daniel: for from the first day that thou didst set thine heart to understand, and to chasten thyself before thy God, thy words were heard, and I am come for thy words" (verses 11, 12).

Royal Honor to Daniel

What great honor is shown to Daniel by the Majesty of heaven! He comforts His trembling servant and assures him that his prayer has been heard in heaven. In answer to that fervent petition the angel Gabriel was sent to affect the heart of the Persian king. The monarch had resisted the impressions of the Spirit of God during the three weeks while Daniel was fasting and praying, but heaven's Prince, the Archangel, Michael, was sent to turn the heart of the stubborn king to take some decided action to answer the prayer of Daniel.

"And when he had spoken such words unto me, I set my face toward the ground, and I became dumb. And, behold, one like the similitude of the sons of men touched my lips. . . . And said, O man greatly beloved, fear not: peace be unto thee, be strong, yea, be strong. And when he had spoken unto me, I was strengthened, and said, Let my lord speak; for thou hast strengthened me" (verses 15-19). So great was the divine glory revealed to Daniel that he could not endure the sight. Then the messenger of heaven veiled the brightness of his presence and appeared to the prophet as "one like the similitude of the sons of men" (verse 16). By his divine power he strengthened this man of integrity and of faith, to hear the message sent to him from God.

Daniel was a devoted servant of the Most High. His long life was filled up with noble deeds of service for his Master. His purity of character and unwavering fidelity are equaled only by his humility of heart and his contrition before God. We repeat, The life of Daniel is an inspired illustration of true sanctification.

20

The Character of John

The apostle John was distinguished above his brethren as "the disciple whom Jesus loved." While not in the slightest degree cowardly, weak, or vacillating in character, he possessed an amiable disposition and a warm, loving heart. He seems to have enjoyed, in a pre-eminent sense, the friendship of Christ, and he received many tokens of the Saviour's confidence and love. He was one of the three permitted to witness Christ's glory upon the mount of transfiguration and His agony in Gethsemane; and to the care of John our Lord confided His mother in those last hours of anguish upon the cross.

The Saviour's affection for the beloved disciple was returned with all the strength of ardent devotion. John clung to Christ as the vine clings to the stately pillar. For his Master's sake he braved the dangers of the judgment hall and lingered about the cross; and at the tidings that Christ had risen, he hastened to the sepulcher, in his zeal outstripping even the impetuous Peter.

John's love for his Master was not a mere human friendship, but it was the love of a repentant sinner, who felt that he had been redeemed by the precious blood of Christ. He esteemed it the highest honor to work and suffer in the service of his Lord. His love for Jesus led him to love all for whom Christ died. His religion was of a practical character. He reasoned that love to God would be manifested in love to His children. He was heard again and again to say, "Beloved, if God so loved us, we ought also to love one another" (1 John 4:11). "We love him, because he first loved us. If a man say, I love God, and hateth his brother, he is a liar: for he that loveth not his brother whom he hath seen, how can he love God whom he hath not seen?" (verses 19,20). The apostle's life was in harmony with his teachings. The love which glowed in his heart for Christ, led him to put forth the most earnest, untiring labor for his fellow men, especially for his brethren in the Christian church. He was a powerful preacher, fervent, and deeply in earnest, and his words carried with them a weight of conviction.

A New Creature Through Grace

The confiding love and unselfish devotion manifested in the life and character of John present lessons of untold value to the Christian church. Some may represent him as possessing this love independent of divine grace; but John had, by nature, serious defects of character; he was proud and ambitious, and quick to resent slight and injury.

The depth and fervor of John's affection for his Master was not the cause of Christ's love for him, but the effect of that love. John desired to become like Jesus, and under the transforming influence of the love of Christ, he became meek and lowly of heart. Self was hid in Jesus. He was closely united to the Living Vine, and thus became a partaker of the divine nature. Such will ever be the result of communion with Christ. This is true sanctification.

There may be marked defects in the character of an individual, yet when he becomes a true disciple of Jesus, the power of divine grace makes him a new creature. Christ's love transforms, sanctifies him. But when persons profess to be Christians, and their religion does not make them better men and better women in all the relations of life—living representatives of Christ in disposition and character—they are none of His.

Lessons in Character Building

At one time John engaged in a dispute with several of his brethren as to which of their number should be accounted greatest. They did not intend their words to reach the ear of the Master; but Jesus read their hearts, and embraced the opportunity to give His disciples a lesson of humility. It was not only for the little group who listened to His words, but was to be recorded for the benefit of all His followers to the close of time. "And he sat down, and called the twelve, and saith unto them, If any man desire to be first, the same shall be last of all, and servant of all" (Mark 9:35).

Those who possess the spirit of Christ will have no ambition to occupy a position above their brethren. It is those who are small in their own eyes who will be accounted great in the sight of God. "And he took a child, and set him in the midst of them: and when he had taken him in his arms, he said unto them, Whosoever shall receive one of such children in my name, receiveth me: and whosoever shall receive me, receiveth not me, but him that sent me" (verses 36, 37).

What a precious lesson is this for all the followers of Christ! Those who overlook the life duties lying directly in their pathway, who neglect mercy and kindness, courtesy and love, to even a little child, are neglecting Christ. John felt the force of this lesson and profited by it.

On another occasion his brother James and himself had seen a man casting out devils in the name of Jesus, and because he did not immediately connect himself with their company, they decided that he had no right to do this work, and consequently forbade him. In the sincerity of his heart John related the circumstance to his Master. Jesus said, "Forbid him not: for there is no man which shall do a miracle in my name, that can lightly speak evil of me. For he that is not against us is on our part" (verses 39, 40).

Again, James and John presented by their mother a petition requesting that they might be permitted to occupy the highest positions of honor in Christ's kingdom. The Saviour answered, "Ye know not what ye ask" (Mark 10:38). How little do many of us understand the true import of our prayers! Jesus knew the infinite sacrifice at which that glory must be purchased, when He, "for the joy that was set before him endured the cross, despising the shame"

(Heb. 12:2). That joy was to see souls saved by His humiliation, His agony, and the shedding of His blood.

This was the glory which Christ was to receive, and which these two disciples had requested that they might be permitted to share. Jesus asked them, "Can ye drink of the cup that I drink of? and be baptized with the baptism that I am baptized with? And they said unto him, We can" (Mark 10:38, 39).

How little did they comprehend what that baptism signified! "Jesus said unto them, Ye shall indeed drink of the cup that I drink of; and with the baptism that I am baptized withal shall ye be baptized: but to sit on my right hand and on my left hand is not mine to give; but it shall be given to them for whom it is prepared" (verses 39, 40).

Pride and Ambition Reproved

Jesus understood the motives which prompted the request, and thus reproved the pride and ambition of the two disciples: "Ye know that they which are accounted to rule over the Gentiles exercise lordship over them; and their great ones exercise authority upon them. But so shall it not be among you: but whosoever will be great among you, shall be your minister: and whosoever of you will be the chiefest, shall be servant of all. For even the Son of man came not to be ministered unto, but to minister, and to give his life a ransom for many" (verses 42-45).

Upon one occasion Christ sent messengers before Him unto a village of the Samaritans, requesting the people to prepare refreshments for Himself and His disciples. But when the Saviour approached the town, He appeared to be passing on toward Jerusalem. This aroused the enmity of the Samaritans, and instead of sending messengers to invite and even urge Him to tarry with them, they withheld the courtesies which they would have given to a common wayfarer. Jesus never urges His presence upon any, and the Samaritans lost the blessing which would have been granted them had they solicited Him to be their guest.

We may wonder at this uncourteous treatment of the Majesty of heaven, but how frequently are we who profess to be the followers of Christ guilty of similar neglect. Do we urge Jesus to take up His abode in our hearts and in our homes? He is full of love, of grace, of blessing, and stands ready to bestow these gifts upon us; but, like the Samaritans, we are often content without them.

The disciples were aware of the purpose of Christ to bless the Samaritans with His presence; and when they saw the coldness, jealousy, and disrespect shown to their Master, they were filled with surprise and indignation. James and John were especially stirred. That He whom they so highly reverenced should be thus treated, seemed to them a crime too great to be passed over without immediate punishment. In their zeal they said, "Lord, wilt thou that we command fire to come down from heaven, and consume them, even as

Elias did?" (Luke 9:54), referring to the destruction of the Syrian captains and their companies sent out to take the prophet Elijah.

Jesus rebuked His disciples, saying, "Ye know not what manner of spirit ye are of. For the Son of man is not come to destroy men's lives, but to save them" (verses 55, 56). John and his fellow disciples were in a school in which Christ was teacher. Those who were ready to see their own defects, and were anxious to improve in character, had ample opportunity. John treasured every lesson and constantly sought to bring his life into harmony with the Divine Pattern. The lessons of Jesus, setting forth meekness, humility, and love as essential to growth in grace, and a fitness for his work, were of the highest value to John. These lessons are addressed to us as individuals and as brethren in the church, as well as to the first disciples of Christ.

John and Judas

An instructive lesson may be drawn from the striking contrast between the character of John and that of Judas. John was a living illustration of sanctification. On the other hand, Judas possessed a form of godliness, while his character was more satanic than divine. He professed to be a disciple of Christ, but in words and in works denied Him.

Judas had the same precious opportunities as had John to study and to imitate the Pattern. He listened to the lessons of Christ, and his character might have been transformed by divine grace. But while John was earnestly warring against his own faults and seeking to assimilate to Christ, Judas was violating his conscience, yielding to temptation, and fastening upon himself habits of dishonesty that would transform him into the image of Satan.

These two disciples represent the Christian world. All profess to be Christ's followers; but while one class walk in humility and meekness, learning of Jesus, the other show that they are not doers of the word, but hearers only. One class are sanctified through the truth; the other know nothing of the transforming power of divine grace. The former are daily dying to self, and are overcoming sin. The latter are indulging their own lusts, and becoming the servants of Satan.

21
The Ministry of John

The apostle John passed his early life in the society of the uncultivated fishermen of Galilee. He did not enjoy the training of the schools; but by association with Christ, the Great Teacher, he obtained the highest education which mortal man can receive. He drank eagerly at the fountain of wisdom, and then sought to lead others to that "well of water springing up into everlasting life" (John 4:14). The simplicity of his words, the sublime power of the truths he uttered, and the spiritual fervor that characterized his teachings gave him access to all classes. Yet even believers were unable to fully comprehend the sacred mysteries of divine truth unfolded in his discourses. He seemed to be constantly imbued with the Holy Spirit. He sought to bring the thoughts of the people up to grasp the unseen. The wisdom with which he spoke, caused his words to drop as the dew, softening and subduing the soul.

After the ascension of Christ, John stands forth a faithful, ardent laborer for the Master. With others he enjoyed the outpouring of the Spirit on the day of Pentecost, and with fresh zeal and power he continued to speak to the people the words of life. He was threatened with imprisonment and death, but he would not be intimidated.

Multitudes of all classes come out to listen to the preaching of the apostles, and are healed of their diseases through the name of Jesus, that name so hated among the Jews. The priests and rulers are frantic in their opposition as they see that the sick are healed and Jesus is exalted as the Prince of life. They fear that soon the whole world will believe on Him, and then accuse them of murdering the Mighty Healer. But the greater their efforts to stop this excitement, the more believe on Him and turn from the teachings of the scribes and Pharisees. They are filled with indignation, and laying hands on Peter and John, thrust them into the common prison. But the angel of the Lord, by night, opens the prison doors, brings them forth, and says, "Go, stand and speak in the temple to the people all the words of this life" (Acts 5:20).

With fidelity and earnestness John bore testimony for his Lord upon every suitable occasion. He saw that the times were full of peril for the church. Satanic delusions were existing everywhere. The minds of the people were wandering through the mazes of skepticism and deceptive doctrines. Some who pretended to be true to the cause of God were deceivers. They denied Christ and His gospel and were bringing in damnable heresies and living in transgression of the divine law.

John's Favorite Theme

John's favorite theme was the infinite love of Christ. He believed in God as a child believes in a kind and tender father. He understood the character and work of Jesus; and when he saw his Jewish brethren groping their way without a ray of the Sun of Righteousness to illuminate their path, he longed to present to them Christ, the Light of the world.

The faithful apostle saw that their blindness, their pride, superstition, and ignorance of the Scriptures were riveting upon their souls fetters which would never be broken. The prejudice and hatred against Christ which they obstinately cherished, was bringing ruin upon them as a nation and destroying their hopes of everlasting life. But John continued to present Christ to them as the only way of salvation. The evidence that Jesus of Nazareth was the Messiah was so clear that John declares no man needs to walk in the darkness of error while such light is proffered him.

Saddened by Poisonous Errors

John lived to see the gospel of Christ preached far and near, and thousands eagerly accepting its teachings. But he was filled with sadness as he perceived poisonous errors creeping into the church. Some who accepted Christ claimed that His love released them from obedience to the law of God. On the other hand, many taught that the letter of the law should be kept, also all the Jewish customs and ceremonies, and that this was sufficient for salvation, without the blood of Christ. They held that Christ was a good man, like the apostles, but denied His divinity. John saw the dangers to which the church would be exposed, should they receive these ideas, and he met them with promptness and decision. He wrote to a most honorable helper in the gospel, a lady of good repute and extensive influence:

"Many deceivers are entered into the world, who confess not that Jesus Christ is come in the flesh. This is a deceiver and an antichrist. Look to yourselves, that we lose not those things which we have wrought, but that we receive a full reward. Whosoever transgresseth, and abideth not in the doctrine of Christ, hath not God. He that abideth in the doctrine of Christ, he hath both the Father and the Son. If there come any unto you, and bring not this doctrine, receive him not into your house, neither bid him God speed: for he that biddeth him God speed is partaker of his evil deeds" (2 John 7-11).

John was not to prosecute his work without great hindrances. Satan was not idle. He instigated evil men to cut short the useful life of this man of God, but holy angels protected him from their assaults. John must stand as a faithful witness for Christ. The church in its peril needed his testimony.

By misrepresentation and falsehood the emissaries of Satan had sought to stir up opposition against John and against the doctrine of Christ. In consequence dissensions and heresies were imperiling the church. John met these errors unflinchingly. He hedged up the way of the adversaries of truth. He wrote and exhorted, that the leaders in these heresies should not have the least encouragement. There are at the present day evils similar to those that threatened the prosperity of the early church, and the teachings of the apostle upon these points should be carefully heeded. "You must have charity," is the cry to be heard everywhere, especially from those who profess sanctification. But charity is too pure to cover an unconfessed sin. John's teachings are important for those who are living amid the perils of the last days. He had been intimately associated with Christ, he had listened to His teachings and had witnessed His mighty miracles. He bore a convincing testimony, which made the falsehoods of His enemies of none effect.

No Compromise With Sin

John enjoyed the blessing of true sanctification. But mark, the apostle does not claim to be sinless; he is seeking perfection by walking in the light of God's countenance. He testifies that the man who professes to know God, and yet breaks the divine law, gives the lie to his profession. "He that saith, I know him, and keepeth not his commandments, is a liar, and the truth is not in him" (1 John 2:4). In this age of boasted liberality these words would be branded as bigotry. But the apostle teaches that while we should manifest Christian courtesy, we are authorized to call sin and sinners by their right names—that this is consistent with true charity. While we are to love the souls for whom Christ died, and labor for their salvation, we should not make a compromise with sin. We are not to unite with the rebellious, and call this charity. God requires His people in this age of the world to stand, as did John in his time, unflinchingly for the right, in opposition to soul-destroying errors.

No Sanctification Without Obedience

I have met many who claimed to live without sin. But when tested by God's word these persons were found to be open transgressors of His holy law. The clearest evidences of the perpetuity and binding force of the fourth commandment failed to arouse the conscience. They could not deny the claims of God, but ventured to excuse themselves in breaking the Sabbath. They claimed to be sanctified, and to serve God on all days of the week. Many good people, they said, did not keep the Sabbath. If men were sanctified, no condemnation would rest upon them if they did not observe it. God was too merciful to punish them for not keeping the seventh day. They would be counted singular in the community should they observe the Sabbath, and would have no influence in the world. And they must be subject to the powers that be.

A lady in New Hampshire bore her testimony in a public meeting that the grace of God was ruling in her heart and that she was wholly the Lord's. She then expressed her belief that this people were doing much good in arousing sinners to see their danger. She said, "The Sabbath that this people present to us is the only Sabbath of the Bible"; and then stated that her mind had been very much exercised upon the subject. She saw great trials before her, which she must meet if she kept the seventh day. The next day she came to meeting and again bore her testimony, saying she had asked the Lord if she must keep the Sabbath, and He had told her she need not keep it. Her mind was now at rest upon that subject. She then gave a most stirring exhortation for all to come to the perfect love of Jesus, where there was no condemnation to the soul.

This woman did not possess genuine sanctification. It was not God who told her that she could be sanctified while living in disobedience to one of His plain commandments. God's law is sacred, and none can transgress it with impunity. The one who told her that she could continue to break God's law and be sinless was the prince of the powers of darkness—the same who told Eve in Eden, through the serpent, "Ye shall not surely die" (Gen. 3:4). Eve flattered herself that God was too kind to punish her for disobedience of His express commands. The same sophistry is urged by thousands in excuse of their disobedience of the fourth commandment. Those who have the mind of Christ will keep all of God's commandments, irrespective of circumstances. The Majesty of heaven says, "I have kept my Father's commandments" (John 15:10).

Adam and Eve dared to transgress the Lord's requirements, and the terrible result of their sin should be a warning to us not to follow their example of disobedience. Christ prayed for His disciples in these words: "Sanctify them through thy truth: thy word is truth" (John 17:17). There is no genuine sanctification except through obedience to the truth. Those who love God with all the heart will love all His commandments also. The sanctified heart is in harmony with the precepts of God's law; for they are holy, just, and good.

God Has Not Changed

God's character has not changed. He is the same jealous God today as when He gave His law upon Sinai and wrote it with His own finger on the tables of stone. Those who trample upon God's holy law may say, "I am sanctified"; but to be indeed sanctified, and to claim sanctification, are two different things.

The New Testament has not changed the law of God. The sacredness of the Sabbath of the fourth commandment is as firmly established as the throne of Jehovah. John writes: "Whosoever committeth sin transgresseth also the law: for sin is the transgression of the law. And ye know that he was manifested to take away our sins; and in him is no sin. Whosoever abideth in him sinneth not: whosoever sinneth (transgresseth the law) hath not seen him, neither known him" (1 John 3: 4-6). We are authorized to hold in the same estimation as did the beloved disciple those who claim to abide in Christ, to be sanctified, while living in transgression of God's law. He met with just such a class as we have to meet. He said, "Little children, let no man deceive you: he that doeth righteousness is righteous, even as he is righteous. He that committeth sin is of the devil; for the devil sinneth from the beginning" (verses 7, 8). Here the apostle speaks in plain terms, as he deemed the subject demanded.

The epistles of John breathe a spirit of love. But when he comes in contact with that class who break the law of God and yet claim that they are living without sin, he does not hesitate to warn them of their fearful deception. "If we say that we have fellowship with him, and walk in darkness, we lie, and do not the truth: but if we walk in the light, as he is in the light, we have fellowship one with another, and the blood of Jesus Christ His Son cleanseth us from all sin. If we say that we have no sin, we deceive ourselves, and the truth is not in us. If we confess our sins, he is faithful and just to forgive us our sins, and to cleanse us from all unrighteousness. If we say that we have not sinned, we make him a liar, and his word is not in us" (1 John 1:6-10).

22

John in Exile

The wonderful success which attended the preaching of the gospel by the apostles and their fellow laborers increased the hatred of the enemies of Christ. They made every effort to hinder its progress, and finally succeeded in enlisting the power of the Roman emperor against the Christians. A terrible persecution ensued, in which many of the followers of Christ were put to death. The apostle John was now an aged man, but with great zeal and success he continued to preach the doctrine of Christ. He had a testimony of power, which his adversaries could not controvert, and which greatly encouraged his brethren.

When the faith of the Christians would seem to waver under the fierce opposition they were forced to meet, the apostle would repeat, with great dignity, power, and eloquence, "That which was from the beginning, which we have heard, which we have seen with our eyes, which we have looked upon, and our hands have handled, of the Word of life; . . . that which we have seen and heard declare we unto you, that ye also may have fellowship with us: and truly our fellowship is with the Father, and with his Son Jesus Christ" (1 John 1:1-3).

The bitterest hatred was kindled against John for his unwavering fidelity to the cause of Christ. He was the last survivor of the disciples who were intimately connected with Jesus, and his enemies decided that his testimony must be silenced. If this could be accomplished, they thought the doctrine of Christ would not spread; and if treated with severity, it might soon die out of the world. John was accordingly summoned to Rome to be tried for his faith. His doctrines were misstated. False witnesses accused him as a seditious person, publicly teaching theories which would subvert the nation.

The apostle presented his faith in a clear and convincing manner, with such simplicity and candor that his words had a powerful effect. His hearers were astonished at his wisdom and eloquence. But the more convincing his testimony, the deeper the hatred of those who opposed the truth. The emperor was filled with rage, and blasphemed the name of God and of Christ. He could not controvert the apostle's reasoning or match the power which attended the utterance of truth, and he determined to silence its faithful advocate.

God's Witness Not Silenced

Here we see how hard the heart may become when obstinately set against the purposes of God. The foes of the church were determined to maintain their pride and power before the people. By the emperor's decree, John was banished to the Isle of Patmos, condemned, as he tells us, "for the word of God, and for the testimony of Jesus Christ" (Rev. 1:9). But the enemies of Christ utterly failed in their purpose to silence His faithful witness. From his place of exile comes the apostle's voice, reaching even to the end of time, proclaiming the most thrilling truths ever presented to mortals.

Patmos, a barren rocky island in the Aegean Sea, had been chosen by the Roman government as a place of banishment for criminals. But to the servant of God this gloomy abode proved to be the gate of heaven. He was shut away from the busy scenes of life and from active labor as an evangelist, but he was not excluded from the presence of God. In his desolate home he could commune with the King of kings and study more closely the manifestations of divine power in the book of nature and the pages of inspiration. He delighted to meditate upon the great work of creation and to adore the power of the Divine Architect. In former years his eyes had been greeted with the sight of wood-covered hills, green valleys, and fruitful plains; and in all the beauties of nature he had delighted to trace the wisdom and skill of the Creator. He was now surrounded with scenes that to many would appear gloomy and uninteresting. But to John it was otherwise. He could read the most important lessons in the wild, desolate rocks, the mysteries of the great deep, and the glories of the firmament. To him all bore the impress of God's power and declared His glory.

The Voice of Nature

The apostle beheld around him the witnesses of the Flood, which deluged the earth because the inhabitants ventured to transgress the law of God. The rocks, thrown up from the great deep and from the earth by the breaking forth of the waters, brought vividly to his mind the terrors of that awful outpouring of God's wrath.

But while all that surrounded him below appeared desolate and barren, the blue heavens that bent above the apostle on lonely Patmos were as bright and beautiful as the skies above his own loved Jerusalem. Let man once look upon the glory of the heavens in the night season and mark the work of God's power in the hosts thereof, and he is taught a lesson of the greatness of the Creator in contrast with his own littleness. If he has cherished pride and self-importance because of wealth, or talents, or personal attractions, let him go out in the beautiful night and look upon the starry heavens, and learn to humble his proud spirit in the presence of the Infinite One.

In the voice of many waters—deep calling unto deep—the prophet heard the voice of the Creator. The sea, lashed to fury by the merciless winds, represented to him the wrath of an offended God. The mighty waves, in their most terrible commotion restrained within the limits appointed by an invisible hand, spoke to John of an infinite power controlling the deep. And in contrast he saw and felt the folly of feeble mortals, but worms of the dust, who glory in their wisdom and strength and set their hearts against the Ruler of the universe, as though God were altogether such a one as themselves. How blind and senseless is human pride! One hour of God's blessing in the sunshine and rain upon the earth will do more to change the face of nature than man with all his

boasted knowledge and persevering efforts can accomplish during a lifetime.
In the surroundings of his island home the exiled prophet read the manifestations of divine power, and in all the works of nature held communion
with his God. The most ardent longing of the soul after God, the most fervent
prayers, went up to heaven from rocky Patmos. As John looked upon the
rocks, he was reminded of Christ, the rock of his strength, in whose shelter he
could hide without a fear.

A Sabbathkeeper

The Lord's day mentioned by John was the Sabbath, the day on which
Jehovah rested after the great work of creation, and which He blessed and
sanctified because He had rested upon it. The Sabbath was as sacredly ob-
served by John upon the Isle of Patmos as when he was among the people,
preaching upon that day. By the barren rocks surrounding him, John was
reminded of rocky Horeb, and how, when God spoke His law to the people
there, He said, "Remember the sabbath day, to keep it holy" (Ex. 20:8).
The Son of God spoke to Moses from the mountain-top. God made the
rocks His sanctuary. His temple was the everlasting hills. The Divine Legisla-
tor descended upon the rocky mountain to speak His law in the hearing of all
the people, that they might be impressed by the grand and awful exhibition of
His power and glory, and fear to transgress His commandments. God spoke
His law amid thunders and lightnings and the thick cloud upon the top of the
mountain, and His voice was as the voice of a trumpet exceeding loud. The
law of Jehovah was unchangeable, and the tablets upon which He wrote that
law were solid rock, signifying the immutability of His precepts. Rocky Horeb
became a sacred place to all who loved and revered the law of God.

Shut in With God

While John was contemplating the scenes of Horeb, the Spirit of Him who
sanctified the seventh day came upon him. He contemplated the sin of Adam
in transgressing the divine law, and the fearful result of that transgression. The
infinite love of God, in giving His Son to redeem a lost race, seemed too great
for language to express. As he presents it in his epistle he calls upon the
church and the world to behold it. "Behold, what manner of love the Father
hath bestowed upon us, that we should be called the sons of God: therefore the
world knoweth us not, because it knew him not" (1 John 3:1). It was a mystery
to John that God could give His Son to die for rebellious man. And he was lost
in amazement that the plan of salvation, devised at such a cost to Heaven,
should be refused by those for whom the infinite sacrifice had been made.

John was shut in with God. As he learned more of the divine character
through the works of creation, his reverence for God increased. He often asked
himself, Why do not men, who are wholly dependent upon God, seek to be at

peace with Him by willing obedience? He is infinite in wisdom, and there is no limit to His power. He controls the heavens with their numberless worlds. He preserves in perfect harmony the grandeur and beauty of the things which He has created. Sin is the transgression of God's law, and the penalty of sin is death. There would have been no discord in heaven or in the earth if sin had never entered. Disobedience to God's law has brought all the misery that has existed among His creatures. Why will not men be reconciled to God?

It is no light matter to sin against God, to set the perverse will of man in opposition to the will of his Maker. It is for the best interest of men, even in this world, to obey God's commandments. And it is surely for their eternal interest to submit to God, and be at peace with Him. The beasts of the field obey their Creator's law in the instinct which governs them. He speaks to the proud ocean, "Hitherto shalt thou come, but no further" (Job 38:11); and the waters are prompt to obey His word. The planets are marshaled in perfect order, obeying the laws which God has established. Of all the creatures that God has made upon the earth, man alone is rebellious. Yet he possesses reasoning powers to understand the claims of the divine law and a conscience to feel the guilt of transgression and the peace and joy of obedience. God made him a free moral agent, to obey or disobey. The reward of everlasting life—an eternal weight of glory—is promised to those who do God's will, while the threatenings of His wrath hang over all who defy His law.

The Majesty of God

As John meditated upon the glory of God displayed in His works, he was overwhelmed with the greatness and majesty of the Creator. Should all the inhabitants of this little world refuse obedience to God, He would not be left without glory. He could sweep every mortal from the face of the earth in a moment, and create a new race to people it and glorify His name. God is not dependent on man for honor. He could marshal the starry hosts of heaven, the millions of worlds above, to raise a song of honor and praise and glory to their Creator. "The heavens shall praise thy wonders, O Lord: thy faithfulness also in the congregation of the saints. For who in the heaven can be compared unto the Lord? who among the sons of the mighty can be likened unto the Lord? God is greatly to be feared in the assembly of the saints, and to be had in reverence of all them that are about him" (Ps. 89:5-7).

A Vision of Christ

John calls to remembrance the wonderful incidents that he has witnessed in the life of Christ. In imagination he again enjoys the precious opportunities with which he was once favored, and is greatly comforted. Suddenly his meditation is broken in upon; he is addressed in tones distinct and clear. He turns to see from whence the voice proceeds, and, lo! he beholds his Lord, whom he has loved, with whom he has walked and talked, and whose sufferings upon the cross he has witnessed. But how changed is the Saviour's appearance! He is no longer "a man of sorrows, and acquainted with grief" (Isa. 53:3). He bears no marks of His humiliation. His eyes are like a flame of fire; His feet like fine brass, as it glows in a furnace. The tones of His voice are like the musical sound of many waters. His countenance shines like the sun in its meridian glory. In His hand are seven stars, representing the ministers of the churches. Out of His mouth issues a sharp, two-edged sword, an emblem of the power of His word.

John, who has so loved his Lord, and who has steadfastly adhered to the truth in the face of imprisonment, stripes, and threatened death, cannot endure the excellent glory of Christ's presence, and falls to the earth as one stricken dead. Jesus then lays His hand upon the prostrate form of His servant, saying, "Fear not; . . . I am he that liveth, and was dead; and, behold, I am alive for evermore" (Rev. 1:17, 18). John was strengthened to live in the presence of his glorified Lord, and then were presented before him in holy vision the purposes of God for future ages. The glorious attractions of the heavenly home were made known to him. He was permitted to look upon the throne of God, and to behold the white-robed throng of redeemed ones. He heard the music of heavenly angels, and the songs of triumph from those who had overcome by the blood of the Lamb and the word of their testimony.

John's Humility

To the beloved disciple were granted such exalted privileges as have rarely been vouchsafed to mortals. Yet so closely had he become assimilated to the character of Christ that pride found no place in his heart. His humility did not consist in a mere profession; it was a grace that clothed him as naturally as a garment. He ever sought to conceal his own righteous acts and to avoid everything that would seem to attract attention to himself. In his Gospel, John mentions the disciple whom Jesus loved, but conceals the fact that the one thus honored was himself. His course was devoid of selfishness. In his daily life he taught and practiced charity in the fullest sense. He had a high sense of the love that should exist among natural brothers and Christian brethren. He presents and urges this love as an essential characteristic of the followers of Jesus. Destitute of this, all pretensions to the Christian name are vain.

John was a teacher of practical holiness. He presents unerring rules for the conduct of Christians. They must be pure in heart and correct in manners. In no case should they be satisfied with an empty profession. He declares in unmistakable terms that to be a Christian is to be Christlike.

The life of John was one of earnest effort to conform to the will of God. The apostle followed his Saviour so closely, and had such a sense of the purity and exalted holiness of Christ, that his own character appeared, in contrast, exceedingly defective. And when Jesus in His glorified body appeared to John, one glimpse was enough to cause him to fall down as one dead. Such will ever be the feelings of those who know best their Lord and Master. The more closely they contemplate the life and character of Jesus, the more deeply will they feel their own sinfulness, and the less will they be disposed to claim holiness of heart or to boast of their sanctification.

23

Christian Character

The character of the Christian is shown by his daily life. Said Christ, "Every good tree bringeth forth good fruit; but a corrupt tree bringeth forth evil fruit" (Matt. 7:17). Our Saviour compares Himself to a vine, of which His followers are the branches. He plainly declares that all who would be His disciples must bring forth fruit; and then He shows how they may become fruitful branches. "Abide in me, and I in you. As the branch cannot bear fruit of itself, except it abide in the vine; no more can ye, except ye abide in me" (John 15:4).

The apostle Paul describes the fruit which the Christian is to bear. He says that it "is in all goodness and righteousness and truth" (Eph. 5:9). And again, "The fruit of the Spirit is love, joy, peace, longsuffering, gentleness, goodness, faith, meekness, temperance" (Gal. 5:22, 23). These precious graces are but the principles of God's law carried out in the life.

The law of God is the only true standard of moral perfection. That law was practically exemplified in the life of Christ. He says of Himself, "I have kept my Father's commandments" (John 15:10). Nothing short of this obedience will meet the requirements of God's word. "He that saith he abideth in him ought himself also so to walk, even as he walked" (1 John 2:6). We cannot plead that we are unable to do this, for we have the assurance, "My grace is sufficient for thee" (2 Cor. 12:9). As we look into the divine mirror, the law of God, we see the exceeding sinfulness of sin, and our own lost condition as transgressors. But by repentance and faith we are justified before God, and through divine grace enabled to render obedience to His commandments.

Love for God and Man

Those who have genuine love for God will manifest an earnest desire to know His will and to do it. Says the apostle John, whose epistles treat so fully upon love, "This is the love of God, that we keep his commandments" (1 John 5:3). The child who loves his parents will show that love by willing obedience; but the selfish, ungrateful child seeks to do as little as possible for his parents, while he at the same time desires to enjoy all the privileges granted to the obedient and faithful. The same difference is seen among those who profess to be children of God. Many who know that they are the objects of His love and care, and who desire to receive His blessing, take no delight in doing His will. They regard God's claims upon them as an unpleasant restraint, His commandments as a grievous yoke. But he who is truly seeking for holiness of heart and life delights in the law of God, and mourns only that he falls so far short of meeting its requirements.

We are commanded to love one another as Christ has loved us. He has manifested His love by laying down His life to redeem us. The beloved disciple says that we should be willing to lay down our lives for the brethren. For "every one that loveth him that begat loveth him also that is begotten of him" (verse 1). If we love Christ, we shall love those who resemble Him in life and character. And not only so, but we shall love those who have "no hope," and are "without God in the world" (Eph. 2:12). It was to save sinners that Christ left His home in heaven and came to earth to suffer and to die. For this He toiled and agonized and prayed, until, heartbroken and deserted by those He came to save, He poured out His life on Calvary.

Imitating the Pattern

Many shrink from such a life as our Saviour lived. They feel that it requires too great a sacrifice to imitate the Pattern, to bring forth fruit in good works, and then patiently endure the pruning of God that they may bring forth more fruit. But when the Christian regards himself as only a humble instrument in the hands of Christ, and endeavors to faithfully perform every duty, relying upon the help which God has promised, then he will wear the yoke of Christ and find it easy; then he will bear burdens for Christ, and pronounce them light. He can look up with courage and with confidence, and say, "I know whom I have believed, and am persuaded that he is able to keep that which I have committed unto him" (2 Tim. 1:12).

If we meet obstacles in our path, and faithfully overcome them; if we encounter opposition and reproach, and in Christ's name gain the victory; if we bear responsibilities and discharge our duties in the spirit of our Master—then, indeed, we gain a precious knowledge of His faithfulness and power. We no longer depend upon the experience of others, for we have the witness in ourselves. Like the Samaritans of old, we can say, "We have heard him ourselves, and know that this is indeed the Christ, the Saviour of the world" (John 4:42).

The more we contemplate the character of Christ, and the more we experience of His saving power, the more keenly shall we realize our own weakness and imperfection, and the more earnestly shall we look to Him as our strength and our Redeemer. We have no power in ourselves to cleanse the soul temple from its defilement; but as we repent of our sins against God, and seek pardon through the merits of Christ, He will impart that faith which works by love and purifies the heart. By faith in Christ and obedience to the law of God we may be sanctified, and thus obtain a fitness for the society of holy angels and the white-robed redeemed ones in the kingdom of glory.

Union With Christ Our Privilege

It is not only the privilege but the duty of every Christian to maintain a close union with Christ and to have a rich experience in the things of God. Then his life will be fruitful in good works. Said Christ, "Herein is my Father glorified, that ye bear much fruit" (John 15:8). When we read the lives of men who have been eminent for their piety we often regard their experiences and attainments as far beyond our reach. But this is not the case. Christ died for all; and we are assured in His word that He is more willing to give His Holy Spirit to them that ask Him than are earthly parents to give good gifts to their children. The prophets and apostles did not perfect Christian character by a miracle. They used the means which God had placed within their reach; and all who will put forth the same effort will secure the same results.

Paul's Prayer for the Church

In his letter to the church at Ephesus, Paul sets before them the "mystery of the gospel" (Eph. 6:19), the "unsearchable riches of Christ" (Eph. 3:8), and then assures them of his earnest prayers for their spiritual prosperity:

"I bow my knees unto the Father of our Lord Jesus Christ, . . . that he would grant you, according to the riches of his glory, to be strengthened with might by his Spirit in the inner man; that Christ may dwell in your hearts by faith; that ye, being rooted and grounded in love, may be able to comprehend with all saints what is the breadth, and length, and depth, and height; and to know the love of Christ, which passeth knowledge, that ye might be filled with all the fulness of God" (Eph. 3:14-19).

He writes to his Corinthian brethren also, "to them that are sanctified in Christ Jesus. . . : Grace be unto you, and peace, from God our Father, and from the Lord Jesus Christ. I thank my God always on your behalf, for the grace of God which is given you by Jesus Christ; that in every thing ye are enriched by him, in all utterance, and in all knowledge; even as the testimony of Christ was confirmed in you: so that ye come behind in no gift; waiting for the coming of our Lord Jesus Christ" (1 Cor. 1:2-7). These words are addressed not only to the church at Corinth but to all the people of God to the close of time. Every Christian may enjoy the blessing of sanctification.

The apostle continues in these words: "Now I beseech you, brethren, by the name of our Lord Jesus Christ, that ye all speak the same thing, and that there be no divisions among you; but that ye be perfectly joined together in the same mind, and in the same judgment" (verse 10). Paul would not have appealed to them to do that which was impossible. Unity is the sure result of Christian perfection.

In the Epistle to the Colossians also are set forth the glorious privileges vouchsafed to the children of God. "Since we heard of your faith in Christ Jesus, and of the love which ye have to all the saints, . . . we also, since the day we heard it, do not cease to pray for you, and to desire that ye might be filled with the knowledge of his will in all wisdom and spiritual understanding; that ye might walk worthy of the Lord unto all pleasing, being fruitful in every good work, and increasing in the knowledge of God; strengthened with all might, according to His glorious power, unto all patience and longsuffering with joyfulness" (Col. 1:4-11).

The Standard of Holiness

The apostle himself was endeavoring to reach the same standard of holiness which he set before his brethren. He writes to the Philippians: "What things were gain to me, those I counted loss for Christ. Yea doubtless, and I count all things but loss for the excellency of the knowledge of Christ Jesus my Lord: . . . that I may know him, and the power of his resurrection, and the fellowship of his sufferings, being made conformable unto his death; if by any means I might attain unto the resurrection of the dead. Not as though I had already attained, either were already perfect: but I follow after, if that I may apprehend that for which also I am apprehended of Christ Jesus. Brethren, I count not myself to have apprehended: but this one thing I do, forgetting those things which are behind, and reaching forth unto those things which are before, I press toward the mark for the prize of the high calling of God in Christ Jesus" (Phil. 3:7-14). There is a striking contrast between the boastful, self-righteous claims of those who profess to be without sin, and the modest language of the apostle. Yet it was the purity and faithfulness of his own life that gave such power to his exhortations to his brethren.

The Will of God

Paul did not hesitate to enforce, upon every suitable occasion, the importance of Bible sanctification. He says: "Ye know what commandments we gave you by the Lord Jesus. For this is the will of God, even your sanctification" (1 Thess. 4:2, 3). "Wherefore, my beloved, as ye have always obeyed, not as in my presence only, but now much more in my absence, work out your own salvation with fear and trembling. For it is God which worketh in you both to will and to do of His good pleasure. Do all things without murmurings and disputings: that ye may be blameless and harmless, the sons of God, without rebuke, in the midst of a crooked and perverse nation, among whom ye shine as lights in the world" (Phil. 2:12-15).

He bids Titus instruct the church that while they should trust to the merits of Christ for salvation, divine grace, dwelling in their hearts, will lead to the faithful performance of all the duties of life. "Put them in mind to be subject to principalities and powers, to obey magistrates, to be ready to every good work, to speak evil of no man, to be no brawlers, but gentle, shewing all meekness unto all men. . . . This is a faithful saying, and these things I will that thou affirm constantly, that they which have believed in God might be careful to maintain good works. These things are good and profitable unto men" (Titus 3:1-8).

Paul seeks to impress upon our minds the fact that the foundation of all acceptable service to God, as well as the very crown of the Christian graces, is love; and that only in the soul where love reigns will the peace of God abide. "Put on therefore, as the elect of God, holy and beloved, bowels of mercies, kindness, humbleness of mind, meekness, longsuffering; forbearing one another, and forgiving one another, if any man have a quarrel against any: even as Christ forgave you, so also do ye. And above all these things put on charity, which is the bond of perfectness. And let the peace of God rule in your hearts, to the which also ye are called in one body; and be ye thankful. Let the word of Christ dwell in you richly in all wisdom; teaching and admonishing one another in psalms and hymns and spiritual songs, singing with grace in your hearts to the Lord. And whatsoever ye do in word or deed, do all in the name of the Lord Jesus, giving thanks to God and the Father by him" (Col. 3:12-17).

24

The Christian's Privilege

Many who are sincerely seeking for holiness of heart and purity of life seem perplexed and discouraged. They are constantly looking to themselves, and lamenting their lack of faith; and because they have no faith, they feel that they cannot claim the blessing of God. These persons mistake feeling for faith. They look above the simplicity of true faith, and thus bring great darkness upon their souls. They should turn the mind from self, to dwell upon the mercy and goodness of God and to recount His promises, and then simply believe that He will fulfill His word. We are not to trust in our faith, but in the promises of God. When we repent of our past transgressions of His law, and resolve to render obedience in the future, we should believe that God for Christ's sake accepts us, and forgives our sins.

Darkness and discouragement will sometimes come upon the soul and threaten to overwhelm us, but we should not cast away our confidence. We must keep the eye fixed on Jesus, feeling or no feeling. We should seek to faithfully perform every known duty, and then calmly rest in the promises of God.

The Life of Faith

At times a deep sense of our unworthiness will send a thrill of terror through the soul, but this is no evidence that God has changed toward us, or we toward God. No effort should be made to rein the mind up to a certain intensity of emotion. We may not feel today the peace and joy which we felt yesterday; but we should by faith grasp the hand of Christ, and trust Him as fully in the darkness as in the light.

Satan may whisper, "You are too great a sinner for Christ to save." While you acknowledge that you are indeed sinful and unworthy, you may meet the tempter with the cry, "By virtue of the atonement, I claim Christ as my Saviour. I trust not to my own merits, but to the precious blood of Jesus, which cleanses me. This moment I hang my helpless soul on Christ." The Christian life must be a life of constant, living faith. An unyielding trust, a firm reliance upon Christ, will bring peace and assurance to the soul.

Resisting Temptation

Be not discouraged because your heart seems hard. Every obstacle, every internal foe, only increases your need of Christ. He came to take away the heart of stone, and give you a heart of flesh. Look to Him for special grace to overcome your peculiar faults. When assailed by temptation, steadfastly resist the evil promptings; say to your soul, "How can I dishonor my Redeemer? I have given myself to Christ; I cannot do the works of Satan." Cry to the dear Saviour for help to sacrifice every idol and to put away every darling sin. Let the eye of faith see Jesus standing before the Father's throne, presenting His wounded hands as He pleads for you. Believe that strength comes to you through your precious Saviour.

Viewing With the Eye of Faith

By faith look upon the crowns laid up for those who shall overcome; listen to the exultant song of the redeemed, Worthy, worthy is the Lamb that was slain and hast redeemed us to God! Endeavor to regard these scenes as real. Stephen, the first Christian martyr, in his terrible conflict with principalities and powers and spiritual wickedness in high places exclaimed, "Behold, I see the heavens opened, and the Son of man standing on the right hand of God" (Acts 7:56). The Saviour of the world was revealed to him as looking down from heaven upon him with the deepest interest, and the glorious light of Christ's countenance shone upon Stephen with such brightness that even his enemies saw his face shine like the face of an angel.

If we would permit our minds to dwell more upon Christ and the heavenly world, we should find a powerful stimulus and support in fighting the battles of the Lord. Pride and love of the world will lose their power as we contemplate the glories of that better land so soon to be our home. Beside the loveliness of Christ, all earthly attractions will seem of little worth.

Let none imagine that without earnest effort on their part they can obtain the assurance of God's love. When the mind has been long permitted to dwell only on earthly things, it is a difficult matter to change the habits of thought. That which the eye sees and the ear hears, too often attracts the attention and absorbs the interest. But if we would enter the city of God, and look upon Jesus and His glory, we must become accustomed to beholding Him with the eye of faith here. The words and the character of Christ should be often the subject of our thoughts and of our conversation, and each day some time should be especially devoted to prayerful meditation upon these sacred themes.

Silencing the Spirit

Sanctification is a daily work. Let none deceive themselves with the belief that God will pardon and bless them while they are trampling upon one of His requirements. The willful commission of a known sin silences the witnessing voice of the Spirit and separates the soul from God. Whatever may be the ecstasies of religious feeling, Jesus cannot abide in the heart that disregards the divine law. God will honor those only who honor Him.

"His servants ye are to whom ye obey" (Rom. 6:16). If we indulge anger, lust, covetousness, hatred, selfishness, or any other sin, we become servants of sin. "No man can serve two masters" (Matt. 6:24). If we serve sin, we cannot serve Christ. The Christian will feel the promptings of sin, for the flesh lusteth against the Spirit; but the Spirit striveth against the flesh, keeping up a constant warfare. Here is where Christ's help is needed. Human weakness becomes united to divine strength, and faith exclaims, "Thanks be to God, which giveth us the victory through our Lord Jesus Christ" (1 Cor. 15:57)!

Correct Religious Habits

If we would develop a character which God can accept, we must form correct habits in our religious life. Daily prayer is as essential to growth in grace, and even to spiritual life itself, as is temporal food to physical well-being. We should accustom ourselves to lift the thoughts often to God in prayer. If the mind wanders, we must bring it back; by persevering effort, habit will finally make it easy. We cannot for one moment separate ourselves from Christ with safety. We may have His presence to attend us at every step, but only by observing the conditions which He Himself has laid down.

Religion must be made the great business of life. Everything else should be held subordinate to this. All our powers, of soul, body, and spirit, must be engaged in the Christian warfare. We must look to Christ for strength and grace, and we shall gain the victory as surely as Jesus died for us.

The Value of the Soul

We must come nearer to the cross of Christ. Penitence at the foot of the cross is the first lesson of peace we have to learn. The love of Jesus—who can comprehend it? Infinitely more tender and self-denying than a mother's love! If we would know the value of a human soul, we must look in living faith upon the cross, and thus begin the study which shall be the science and the song of the redeemed through all eternity. The value of our time and our talents can be estimated only by the greatness of the ransom paid for our redemption. What ingratitude do we manifest toward God when we rob Him of His own by withholding from Him our affections and our service! Is it too much to give ourselves to Him who has sacrificed all for us? Can we choose the friendship of the world before the immortal honors which Christ proffers—"to sit with me in my throne, even as I also overcame, and am set down with my Father in his throne" (Rev. 3:21)?

A Progressive Work

Sanctification is a progressive work. The successive steps are set before us in the words of Peter: "Giving all diligence, add to your faith virtue; and to virtue knowledge; and to knowledge temperance; and to temperance patience; and to patience godliness; and to godliness brotherly kindness; and to brotherly kindness charity. For if these things be in you, and abound, they make you that ye shall neither be barren nor unfruitful in the knowledge of our Lord Jesus Christ" (2 Peter 1:5-8). "Wherefore the rather, brethren, give diligence to make your calling and election sure: for if ye do these things, ye shall never fall: for so an entrance shall be ministered unto you abundantly into the everlasting kingdom of our Lord and Saviour Jesus Christ" (verses 10, 11).

Here is a course by which we may be assured that we shall never fall. Those who are thus working upon the plan of addition in obtaining the Christian graces have the assurance that God will work upon the plan of multiplication in granting them the gifts of His Spirit. Peter addresses those who obtained like precious faith: "Grace and peace be multiplied unto you through the knowledge of God, and of Jesus our Lord" (verse 2). By divine grace, all who will may climb the shining steps from earth to heaven, and at last, "with songs and everlasting joy" (Isa. 35:10), enter through the gates into the city of God.

Our Saviour claims all there is of us; He asks our first and holiest thoughts, our purest and most intense affection. If we are indeed partakers of the divine nature, His praise will be continually in our hearts and upon our lips. Our only safety is to surrender our all to Him and to be constantly growing in grace and in the knowledge of the truth.

Paul's Shout of Victory

The apostle Paul was highly honored of God, being taken in holy vision to the third heaven, where he looked upon scenes whose glories he was not permitted to reveal. Yet this did not lead him to boastfulness or self-confidence. He realized the importance of constant watchfulness and self-denial, and plainly declares, "I keep under my body, and bring it into subjection: lest that by any means, when I have preached to others, I myself should be a castaway" (1 Cor. 9:27).

Paul suffered for the truth's sake, and yet we hear no complaints from his lips. As he reviews his life of toil and care and sacrifice, he says, "I reckon that the sufferings of this present time are not worthy to be compared with the glory which shall be revealed in us" (Rom. 8:18). The shout of victory from God's faithful servant comes down the line to our time: "Who shall separate us from the love of Christ? shall tribulation, or distress, or persecution, or famine, or nakedness, or peril, or sword? . . . Nay, in all these things we are more than conquerors through him that loved us. For I am persuaded, that neither death, nor life, nor angels, nor principalities, nor powers, nor things present, nor things to come, nor height, nor depth, nor any other creature, shall be able to separate us from the love of God, which is in Christ Jesus our Lord" (Rom. 8:35-39).

Though Paul was at last confined in a Roman prison—shut away from the light and air of heaven, cut off from his active labors in the gospel, and momentarily expecting to be condemned to death—yet he did not yield to doubt or despondency. From that gloomy dungeon came his dying testimony, full of a sublime faith and courage that has inspired the hearts of saints and martyrs in all succeeding ages. His words fitly describe the results of that sanctification which we have in these pages endeavored to set forth: "I am now ready to be offered, and the time of my departure is at hand. I have fought a good fight, I have finished my course, I have kept the faith: henceforth there is laid up for me a crown of righteousness, which the Lord, the righteous judge, shall give me at that day: and not to me only, but unto all them also that love his appearing" (2 Tim. 4:6-8).

Index to Scripture References

NOTES

NOTES